Collins *practical gardener*

LAWNS

Collins *practical gardener*

LAWNS

MARTIN FISH

First published in 2005 by HarperCollins*Publishers*

77–85 Fulham Palace Road, London, W6 8JB

The Collins website address is:

www.collins.co.uk

Text by Martin Fish; copyright © HarperCollins*Publishers*

Artworks and design © HarperCollins*Publishers*

The majority of photographs in this book were taken by
Tim Sandall. A number of other images were supplied
by David Sarton

Cover photography by Tim Sandall

Photographic props: Coolings Nurseries, Rushmore Hill,
Knockholt, Kent, TN14 7NN, www.coolings.co.uk

Design and editorial: Focus Publishing, Sevenoaks, Kent

Project editor: Guy Croton

Editor: Vanessa Townsend

Project co-ordinator: Caroline Watson

Design & illustration: David Etherington

For HarperCollins

Senior managing editor: Angela Newton

Design manager: Luke Griffin

Editor: Alastair Laing

Assistant editor: Lisa John

Production: Chris Gurney

A CIP catalogue record for this book is available from the
British Library

ISBN 0-00-718266-X

Colour reproduction by Colourscan

Printed and bound in Great Britain by The Bath Press Ltd

Contents

INTRODUCTION

Lawns come in all shapes and sizes, from manicured and striped lawns to tough hardwearing areas of grass. To many, looking after a lawn is a chore and is not considered very important. Yet from a garden design point of view, lawns are very important ,and many people would not consider creating a garden without a lawn of some sort. Although gardening trends come and go, the lawn is definitely here to stay. It provides not only an attractive feature but a surface for play and an area in which to relax in the garden. It also acts as a foil to plants and borders – take away the lawn and the garden would be much less interesting to look at. Even in the middle of winter when the garden can look a little bare, a lawn will always provide some colour.

Despite the importance of lawns, they are often taken for granted and only given the minimum of care. Part of the reason for this is because it is widely believed that to have a good quality lawn you need to spend a great deal of time and money on maintenance. In the case of a golf green or football pitch this may be the case, but for a garden lawn it is possible to create and maintain a lawn in good condition without being a slave to it. Lawn care is also thought to be difficult and a bit of a mystery, but with improved and new varieties of grass and an increasing range of lawn care products, lawn maintenance has never been as easy or enjoyable. A well kept lawn will involve some work, but the results far outweigh the effort and if you treat your lawn as being as important as the rest of the other features and plants in your garden, the whole area will appear to be more aesthetically pleasing to the eye.

This book is aimed at gardeners who appreciate that a lawn is an important part of the garden and for those who want to create a new lawn or maintain and improve an existing one. It is also for those who might want to try something a little different in their garden – a break from tradition. Lawns can be used in many other ways such as for growing wild flowers, lawn sculptures and to create mown shapes to add interest and movement to the garden.

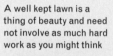

A well kept lawn is a thing of beauty and need not involve as much hard work as you might think

HISTORY OF LAWNS

Lawns have been part of gardens for several hundreds of years, but initially they were only the preserve of those wealthy enough to afford the labour to mow them. If he had a garden at all, the working man would have used the land to grow vegetables, herbs and perhaps a few flowers.

Early lawns

Early lawns were very different to what we know today. Often, they were merely meadows that were occasionally grazed by animals to create areas of shorter grass around buildings. As gardening became more popular in Elizabethan times, lawns became more fashionable and were laid in large numbers around the many country homes that were built during this period. These lawns were either grazed or scythed and would contain a mixture of grasses and other plants such as chamomile that gave off a pleasant fragrance when walked upon. Indeed, the main purpose of many of these lawns was to provide a recreational facility, and scented plants were included to help mask the many unpleasant smells of the time. Short areas of grass were also maintained for the playing of sports such as bowls and pall-mall, which was later renamed croquet.

The invention of the mower

In the 18th century formal lawns became popular on large estates and in order to keep them short they would have been regularly cut with a scythe, sickle or hand shears. A skilled man with a scythe was able to cut the grass very short and even.

However, it was the invention of the first mechanical lawnmower that made lawns more accessible to the general public. An English engineer working in the textile trade based the first mower on a cutter used to trim cloth and in 1830 the idea was patented and the first mowers followed shortly

afterwards, produced by a firm named Ransomes. This first mower had a cutting cylinder and needed to be operated by two men. One would pull and the other push. Soon to follow were smaller and lighter versions that could be used by one person and also larger models that were pulled by horses wearing leather shoes to prevent them from leaving hoof prints on the grass. These horse-drawn mowers were manufactured by a company called Shanks, and their product is thought to be behind the saying 'shanks' pony', meaning to walk. Although the mowers were designed to be pulled by ponies, they were more often pulled by men! By the late 19th century lawns had become an established part of the garden, not only for the rich but also for the working man.

Today, lawns are still very much part of the gardening scene, and thanks to the work carried out by various sporting organizations much of the expertise and technology has worked its way down to garden level. Because grass is so widely used as a sports surface, lawns should continue to flourish.

Early mowers were complex and heavy contraptions that often required more than one operator

The design of the basic cylinder mower has changed very little over the years

MAKING A LAWN

Creating a new lawn from scratch is much easier than you might think and the end result will be very satisfying and rewarding. Lawns can be made from many different types of plants, but the most popular and practical lawn is one made from grass and usually mixtures of different grasses are used to create a thick sward.

Planning the Lawn

Here the lawn is the central feature in a garden full of interest

Before embarking on a new lawn, some planning should be done first. As you are starting to make a lawn from bare earth you have the option to decide exactly what you want. It really is worth thinking about the options because once the lawn is laid and established, to change it can be difficult. When laid properly, a lawn will last a lifetime, so it pays to try and get it right from the onset with minimum effort.

What will the lawn be used for? The main thing to take into account is what the new lawn is mainly going to be used for. It is all too easy to buy the first box of grass seed you find in a garden centre or to order turf from the first supplier you find listed in the telephone book, but before you get to that stage you need to ask yourself why do you want a lawn? Do you want a fine quality

'show' lawn that will rarely be walked upon or a lawn that needs to be able to withstand children and pets running and playing on it? These are completely different types of lawn, and to create each successfully you need different grass mixtures. If you were to use a fine lawn mix and subject it to heavy wear, it would soon be ruined. Likewise, by using a strong grown seed mixture you will never get a fine quality lawn. It is, however, possible to have a hardwearing lawn that also looks good all year round, as long as you use the correct mix of grasses.

Where is the lawn to be sited? You also need to think about the position of the lawn in the garden: what type of soil you need to work with, what level of drainage, whether the area is prone to drought, whether all or part of it will be in shade most of the time, whether it is next to over-hanging trees, and so on – all of these points are covered later on in this book.

How quickly do you want it? There is also the timescale to take into account. Growing a lawn from seed is much slower than establishing turf, so if you need a lawn in a hurry, grass seed will not be the best route to take.

Types of Lawn

There are many different types of lawn that you can create in your garden and you only have to look at the different sports that are played on grass to give you some idea of what they look like and how they can be used. Fortunately, grass seed companies have taken much of the hard work out of choosing what types of grass to use on a lawn and they have blended various grasses together to form different mixtures. These lawn seed mixtures are readily available from garden centres and specialist mail order companies. To a certain extent, the same applies to turf and many companies now sell several different grades of turf to suit all needs. Generally speaking when

choosing seed or turf, you get what you pay for. It is best to avoid very cheap seed mixes where little or no detail of the grass mixture is given.

Although lawn types tend to fall into two main groups, fine-quality and utility lawns, many of the modern seed mixtures available fall midway, enabling you to have an all-purpose lawn that looks fairly fine and also can withstand the wear and tear of children and pets. These contain a selection of fine and hardwearing seed varieties and many seed companies sell such mixtures. Most turf companies also sell good quality turf that is classed as all-purpose for garden use.

Fine-quality show lawns

A fine-quality lawn that is maintained to a high standard always looks impressive. It consists of a mixture of fine-leaved grasses that do not grow too quickly or too tall and ideally the lawn should be weed- and moss-free. The two main types of grass used in a fine mixture are Festuca (fescue) and

A fine-quality lawn will take a mowing stripe better than any other kind

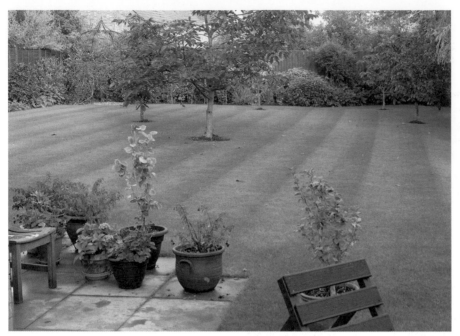

jobs to do and the rewards will be a very good quality lawn that complements the rest of the garden.

Hardwearing lawn

If you want a lawn that looks good all year round and can stand the daily ravages of children and pets, you will need to choose a hard-wearing mixture. These are often known as 'family' or 'utility' mixtures. In the past, this type of lawn would have been largely made up of very vigorous, fast growing ryegrass, but nowadays the new cultivars are much better and, although hardwearing, they have a finer leaf and do not grow as tall.

The main ingredient of a family lawn is *Lolium perenne* (perennial ryegrass) and often it comprises of up to 90% of the mixture. This gives the grass its strength and recovery power after heavy use, hence the reason it is widely used on football and rugby pitches. The remainder of the mixture is usually *Festuca rubra rubra* (creeping red fescue) or *Poa pratensis* (smooth stalked meadow grass) or both, which is used to bind the lawn together. Seed companies offer several mixtures suitable for this type of lawn which establishes very quickly, and turf companies also offer a selection of utility turf.

Maintenance requirements This type of lawn requires less maintenance than a very fine formal lawn, although for best results regular mowing is necessary and ideally the lawn should be fed once or twice a year. A cylinder or rotary mower can be used to cut the grass, which should normally be allowed to grow a little longer due to the nature of its use. Weed and moss control will be required if you want to keep the lawn free from weeds and moss, although a few weeds in this type of lawn are not as noticeable as in a very fine grass mixture.

A fine-quality lawn will look superb if well kept, but will not withstand hard use by children or animals

Agrostis (bent grass) and several cultivars of both may be blended to provide a thick, but fine-leaved sward. These are the types of grasses that you would expect to find on golf greens and bowling greens. This type of lawn can be made by sowing seed, as most seed companies sell a fine lawn mixture, but establishment by this method is not as fast as with other seed mixtures. Alternatively, several of the turf growers produce fine-quality turf.

Unfortunately, the grasses in this type of lawn are not very hardwearing compared with other types and therefore it is not the best choice for a lawn that will get lots of heavy wear from children or pets. However, for normal use it will serve perfectly well.

Maintenance requirements The maintenance of a fine lawn can be quite high if you want to keep it in excellent condition all year round, although regular mowing with a cylinder mower is the main job. Apart from regular mowing, you will need to feed the lawn a couple of times a year, and control weeds and moss to keep it looking really good. It may also be necessary to carry out other maintenance such as spiking or scarifying from time to time. All this might sound daunting, but in reality these are easy

Creating a Non-Grass Lawn

The majority of lawns are grown with grasses, but in some situations other plants may be used as an alternative. The use of non-grass species in lawns goes back to Elizabethan times when many herbs such as chamomile were used in lawns to create a sweet smelling fragrance when walked upon. Pennyroyal was also used as part of a lawn to help deter fleas and other insects. Even today many very old, established lawns around country houses have a mixture of chamomile and grass in the lawn.

The pleasures of a non-grass lawn lie in the different fragrances that many of the plants give off, their coloured foliage and, in some cases, attractive flowers that help to attract wildlife into the garden.

Where to site? Non-grass lawns work well in courtyards or other places where lawn mower access is difficult, or around the base of a tree or garden sculptures where you want something a little different. Many plants will tolerate being mown occasionally and are ideal for creating small areas of lawn where grass is not wanted, but most of the plants used will not stand heavy traffic and such a lawn will only really work as an ornamental feature. They will never be a substitute for a grass lawn but it is fun to have a small area in the garden and they are guaranteed to be a talking point.

Suitable plants for a non-grass lawn

Thyme (Thymus)
Chamomile (*Chamaemelum nobilis*)
Pennyroyal (*Mentha pulegium*)
Clover (Trifolium)
Mixed low-growing alpines
  – for example, Saxifrage (Saxifraga) and Pratia

Maintenance requirements The main disadvantage in a non-grass lawn is that the maintenance can be quite intensive during the early stages of establishment. Weeds can be a problem until the plants grow together, and as there are no selective weedkillers available for use on broad-leaved plants, hand weeding is the only solution. However, as the plants establish and form a dense mat, weeds will become less of a problem. Mowing only needs to be undertaken once or twice a year to keep the plants in trim.

Laying a non-grass lawn

Ground preparation is very important when laying an area of non-grass lawn in order to prevent invasion by perennial weeds at a later date. As the area being created is usually quite small, this should not present too much of a problem.

TIP
If you do not fancy the hard graft of forking out perennial roots, an alternative is to spray the weeds with a glyphosate-based weedkiller. This is absorbed into the plant, killing all parts including the roots. Once the weeds are dead, the ground can be forked over to loosen the soil. Glyphosate does not leave any harmful residues in the soil.

Chamomile makes a soft, deliciously aromatic alternative lawn

Preparing the soil Annual weeds can simply be lifted or, in sunny weather, dislodged with a hoe and left to dry out. With perennial weeds, it is vital to remove all pieces of root, as many will re-grow from even the tiniest fragment. The old-fashioned and totally organic way to do this is to fork over the soil and pick out the roots by hand.

Once the site is completely clear of weeds, rake down the soil to form a level surface and apply a base dressing of general fertilizer. This should be lightly raked into the soil surface. The site is now ready to plant or sow.

Digging out weeds using a fork before they establish themselves and over-run the non-grass lawn helps to remove all of the root system

1

2

3

Planting The best time to establish a non-grass lawn is in early autumn or spring. Plants such as chamomile, thyme and alpines are usually available as established plants in small pots, although some nurseries will supply smaller plants in large plug trays.

1 – Where established plants are being used it may be possible to divide the clump into several rooted sections. This not only saves money, but also the plants will go further.

2 – Space the plants out in staggered rows and plant them approximately 15–20cm (6–8 in) apart. Wider spacing can be used, but it will take longer for the plants to grow together.

3 – Water the plants thoroughly to settle them in and keep the soil around them moist in dry weather until they are established.

Sowing A few plants such as clover and thyme can be grown from seed, although thyme is often established from small plants. This is best done in spring when the soil is starting to warm up. The ground needs preparing thoroughly and raking down to form a firm seed bed. Broadcast the seeds evenly over the area and lightly rake them into the surface – just as you would with grass seed. Germination can be a little slow, especially in dry weather. If this is the case, water the area with a watering can or sprinkler to keep the soil moist.

Aftercare and maintenance

Once established a non-grass lawn needs very little attention, but while the plants are establishing you will need to keep an eye on them to ensure that they take hold.

Weeding Any perennial weeds that were missed when the ground was being prepared should be carefully lifted as they grow, otherwise they will quickly establish themselves and smother the plants. The seeds of annual weeds will also appear between the plants and these should either be hoed off or pulled out by hand. In dry weather keep the young plants watered to prevent them from drying out and pinch out any upward growing shots to encourage bushy growth. In good growing conditions plants should grow and spread quickly to form a solid mat within several weeks. This of course will depend on the vigour of the individual plants and the spaces between them when they were planted. Any weeds that do manage to grow through the plants should be removed by hand as soon as they are seen, although when the plants are established to form a thick ground cover it becomes difficult for most weeds to grow.

Use liquid feeds annually to help grass and non-grass lawns at the start of the growing season

Feeding Once established, feed the plants once a year in spring with a general fertilizer to start them into growth for the season. Remember that lawn weed and feed cannot be used on non-grass lawns, as the selective weedkiller in the product will kill broad-leaved plants.

Mowing The amount of trimming needed on a non-grass area will depend on the type of plants being used, but generally no more than a couple of light trimmings per year are required. A spring trim tidies up the plants after winter and a late summer trim removes any taller shoots and old flower stems. This can be done with a rotary mower on a high setting, with a nylon cord strimmer or by hand shears. For small areas, hand shears give a neater finish.

Sedum 'paving'

Another plant that is becoming popular for non-grass lawn areas is sedum. This is a small hardy plant with succulent leaves that is available in many species to give year-round interest.

Laying sedum 'paving'

It you want to break up a large expanse of paving, it is possible to lift a few slabs and establish a small area of non-grass lawn – a few small areas of greenery on a patio will make all the difference. Sedum is ideal for this because it will grow in virtually no soil and you can buy ready-made mats for just this purpose.

1 – Lift a paving slab and remove any loose concrete.

2 – Add a thin layer of soil or gritty, well-drained compost to the level of the surrounding paving. It can be as little as 2.5cm (1in) in depth.

3 – Lay the sedum mat on the soil, trim to get a good fit and water in.

4 – Your new sedum mat will firmly establish itself in no time.

Designing a Lawn

As part of the overall design of a garden, a lawn plays a very important role, regardless of whether it is purely for decoration, for a children's play area or a space for entertaining and relaxing. If you are in a position where the entire garden is being designed or laid out from scratch, you can create a lawn of any shape to suit the garden. Likewise, existing lawns within an established garden can be altered and re-shaped to give the garden a new look. Whatever shape or size of lawn you go for, it should fit in with the rest of the garden.

Think of the lawns as the carpet in your living room and the plants as the furniture – both equally important and there to complement each other.

How will the lawn be used? As already mentioned, when designing a lawn it is essential that you take into account how the lawn will be used. For example, if you have children who want to kick a ball around the lawn needs to be spacious, but on the other hand if you mainly want your garden to contain plants, the lawn can be used as a foil to set off the beauty of the plants and the shape of the beds and borders, or to link areas together, forming paths between beds and borders.

What kind of house do you have?
Another key consideration when creating a lawn is the style that you are looking to achieve. This can be influenced by several factors but one of the most important is the location of the house. For example, small town gardens quite often fill the limited space with a formal lawn in order to maximize the potential for sitting out and playing. Yet this can also make the garden look smaller, and often a curved or meandering lawn in a small garden will give the illusion of space. On the other hand, a detached house with an extensive garden space can provide an opportunity for a large formal lawn, but if it is too large it can look intimidating. A better choice, perhaps, would be to divide the garden into different areas, including both formal and informal lawns, especially if you are trying to achieve a relaxed, cottage garden feel.

What features do you require? You also need to think about other features within the garden such as paths and paving, garden

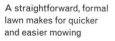

A straightforward, formal lawn makes for quicker and easier mowing

furniture, beds and borders, ponds and vegetables plot. If you intend to create some hard-landscaped areas, it is better to try and do these before the lawn is laid to prevent damage and compaction to the grass. Ideally, when creating a whole garden, the lawn should be the last job.

Dealing with obstructions Large trees, hedges and tall walls also need to be taken into account, as they may cast shadows onto the lawn. A small amount of shade is not too much of a problem, but heavy shade can spoil a lawn (see Aspect, page 19). Manholes or inspection chambers can also be a nuisance, especially in new properties. Where possible they should be disguised by some planting or a large container. If left as part of a lawn they will be very obvious and the first thing you see when you look out onto the lawn.

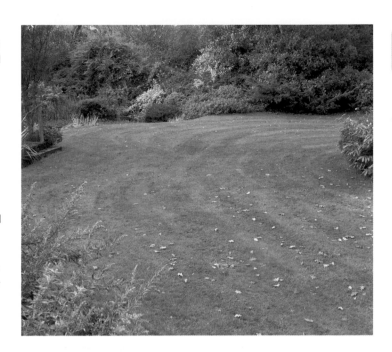

TIP
A disadvantage with a square or rectangular lawn is that it can make the garden look too 'blocky'. One way of overcoming this is to set the lawn diagonally so that you still have a rectangular lawn, but in doing so have created more interest and different shaped planting pockets around the lawn.

Of course there are no hard-and-fast rules when it comes to the shape and style of a lawn and at the end of the day the choice is yours. The good thing about a lawn is that it can easily be changed if you decide that you want to alter it at a later date. This is often the case when you want to introduce new plants into the garden or because existing plants are becoming larger and encroaching onto the lawn.

Formal lawns

A formal lawn is usually square, rectangular or circular and very often symmetrical. It may have a formal bed in the middle or be surrounded by formal borders. From a maintenance point of view lawns with straight edges are easier and faster to mow, so if mowing time is an issue a formal lawn may be worth considering. However, when

you have straight edges it is important that they are well maintained by regular trimming and kept straight. Although any type of mower can be used to cut the grass, for maximum effect use a mower with a roller to produce stripes up and down the lawn.

Informal lawns

An informal lawn consists of curves that meander gently around the garden. Straight lines are a definite no-no. The lawn can be any shape that you want and within the lawn there can be informal-shaped beds. The aim is to create a natural-looking shape that complements the mixed planting around it. Very often the curves of the lawn are designed to lead your eye along the garden to a focal point in the distance. When forming the shape of the lawn, try to avoid tight, fussy curves as these not only look unnatural, but are also more difficult to mow; one large sweeping curve is much more effective than several small scallop-shaped curves. As for mowing time, an informal lawn of the same area as a formal lawn will probably take a little longer to mow due to the fact that you often mow over some parts of the lawn more than once because of the shape.

Informal, curved lawns or those adorned with features are much harder to mow

Paths & Edging

In any garden you need to be able to get from one point to another – either between different areas of the garden or from the garden to the house and the world outside. There are many different types of material that can be laid across or around a lawn to form a path. The material you select will depend on what the path is going to be used for. It is even possible to continue the lawn theme by creating a grass path to run across those areas of the garden that are not covered by actual lawn.

Grass paths

Grass paths look very natural and are lovely to stroll along on a summer's day. They are also an ideal way of linking two areas of the garden together, of dissecting a large bed or dividing a kitchen garden into smaller plots. Maintenance is very simple and just involves keeping the grass mown and tidy. They are also easy to create and in many cases can evolve from an existing lawn.

Creating a grass path If you want to create a new grass path either seed or turf can be used, although turf is much faster to establish than seed, meaning that the path can be used almost immediately after laying. Choose a turf with strong-growing rye-grass in the mixture to prevent wear and tear, and make the path no less than 1m (3ft) wide as very narrow paths can be impractical to mow

A paving slab and brick path is durable and good looking but relatively expensive to install

and maintain. Ideally the path should be wide enough for two people to walk side by side.

Disadvantages The main disadvantage of a grass path is that the grass can quickly wear in some situations. When there is heavy foot traffic the grass can easily become bare and in winter the path can turn into a mud bath when used on a regular basis. If this is the case then perhaps a grass path is not the answer and you need to consider an alternative.

Solid paving

The hardest wearing materials for paths that require the least maintenance are concrete or paving slabs, although the latter are the more decorative as there are many attractive slabs available. These will form a hard surface that is accessible all year round. The path should be laid on a 75mm (3in) base of compacted crushed-stone (usually sold as hardcore or road-stone), and when finished the paving slabs should be positioned just below the level of the grass to make mowing easier. For a firmer and more level base to the slabs, add a 35–50mm (1–2in) level of sharp sand on top of the crushed stone layer, though many gardeners find this is not strictly necessary and it does involve digging out more soil.

Gravel paths

A cheaper and easily laid garden path can be made with gravel or decorative chippings. This type of path can look very natural and give a softer appearance than a concrete or slab path. Gravel is hardwearing, can be walked on regardless of the weather and is very good from a security point of view – try walking on gravel without making a noise!

For general garden use where you walk occasionally or push a wheelbarrow, there is no need to lay a foundation for the path as the gravel will carry the weight on its own. For heavy, regular use, a crushed-stone base of approximately 10–15cm (4–6in) will make the path much firmer, but this will involve the removal of a great deal of soil.

1

Laying a gravel path

1 – Dig out the area where you want the path to be to a depth of approximately 10cm (4in). Use a string line to mark out a straight path or a hose pipe to shape a curved one.

2 – Line the sides of the path with lengths of treated timber – 10cm (4in) deep – held in position with wooden pegs so that the timber boards are just below the lawn.

3 – Lay landscape fabric across the base of the path. This will prevent perennial weeds growing up through the gravel and stop the gravel treading into the soil base.

4 – Finish off with a layer of gravel no thicker than 5cm (2in). Any deeper and it is difficult to walk on and the aim is to keep the path lower than the lawn for mowing purposes.

2

3

4

Stepping stones

Stepping stones across a lawn are ideal where a solid path is not required, but where grass on its own is not enough. When properly spaced and laid the stepping stones will carry all the weight and the lawn will not be damaged. An advantage of stepping stones is they are fast and easy to install, and if you want to remove them at a later date they can simply be lifted and the small bare areas they leave behind can be patched in with turf.

1 – Once the slabs are evenly spaced cut carefully around each one with a with a half-moon edging iron.

2 – Lift the piece of turf with a spade and scrape out any loose soil so that the depth of the hole is a little deeper than the slab.

3 – Add some sharp sand into the base of the hole to form a flat level surface to bed the slab onto.

4 – Position the slab into the hole and gently firm it down onto the sand. When finished, the slab should be just lower than the grass for ease of mowing.

1

2

3

Lawn edges

There are several reasons for having a solid edge to a lawn. If your soil is very light, a solid edge will maintain the edge and prevent it from crumbling away. There are various types of edging strips made from plastic or metal widely available on the market and when installed they are more or less invisible. Metal edges in lengths that lock together are the strongest of all and will last for many years. They are maintenance-free and can be fitted to both straight and curved edges. Be sure to fit edgings accurately at the outset for them to look their best.

1

2

3

Laying brick edging An edging made from bricks offers a more decorative and solid appearance than edging strips. It will also serve as a mowing strip, enabling you to mow right to the edge of the lawn, as you can run the mower's wheels over the bricks provided they are correctly sunk to a level just below that of the grass. The presence of a mowing strip does away completely with the need to trim the lawn edges with long-handled shears.

1 – Dig out a trench along the edge of the lawn the width of the brick and approximately twice its depth.

2 – Make a concrete mix using one part cement and four parts sharp sand or ballast and thoroughly line the base of the trench with the mix.

3 – Position the bricks on the concrete and gently tap them down using the handle of a pound hammer or a rubber mallet, until they are positioned just below the surface of the grass.

Temporary paths

Sometimes you may need to walk or to push a wheelbarrow across an area of the lawn more than usual, and in wet conditions this could damage the lawn and churn up the grass. For the few occasions when this is likely to happen there is no point laying a permanent path, but if possible you should try to protect the lawn. One way is to have a temporary, portable path. Plastic roll-out paths can be bought or you can make your own from short pieces of wood fastened to lengths of thick string. The path is simply rolled out when you need it and rolled away when you have finished crossing the lawn. Remember, though, that this type of path should only be left on the lawn for a few days, as otherwise the lawn will start to turn yellow where the path is laid.

Timber boards can also be installed around the perimeter of a lawn to prevent the edges from crumbling, or as a barrier between a lawn and gravel path. The timber should be pressure-treated as untreated wood will rot in a few years as a result of being constantly moist. Boards 2.5cm (1in) thick and 7.5cm (3in) deep, set so that they are just below the surface of the lawn, will provide a solid edge that will last for many years.

A brick edging is both decorative and functional, as it will serve as a mowing strip, saving on edge trimming

Assessing Your Garden

Grasses, just like other plants, need the correct conditions in order to grow well, although sometimes the site of a lawn is given little consideration. This is often the case with new properties, where lawns are laid directly onto ground that is compacted and full of building waste. Although many types of grass are tolerant of different conditions and will adapt to their environment, for a lawn to look good throughout the year and to be healthy, some thought needs to be given to the site, and not just the design of the lawn.

Generally speaking, a lawn will thrive in most fertile, well-drained soils that receive sun for part of the day.

In most gardens, it is possible to grow a lawn if you want one, but likewise there are usually some areas of the garden where conditions are less favourable. In these areas more thought needs to be given to the site preparation and selection of grass types. If you prepare correctly, you will be able to produce a lawn of reasonable quality, but if not the lawn will struggle to establish and will never really be satisfactory. Fortunately, the range of different grasses available to gardeners means that a lawn can be grown in most situations without too many problems.

Aspect

The aspect of a garden is not very often taken into account when a lawn is being laid, but it is actually of some importance. For example, a garden that is in full sun for most of the day will produce a lawn that is completely different to one that is in shade.

When deciding on the position of a lawn, make a note of where the sun rises and sets and mark out any parts of the garden that will be in total shade for part or all of the day. The amount of sun falling on the garden will be influenced by buildings, walls, fences and tall trees. If you find that the garden receives a mixture of sun and shade throughout the day, this is not a problem and you should be able to grow any type of lawn. If the aspect is very hot and sunny, you should experience few problems, but it is worth choosing a seed or turf mixture that contains grasses tolerant of heat and drought, such as creeping red fescue and smooth-stalked meadow grass. If, on the other hand, the area is in shade for most of the day, a mixture that contains hard fescue and creeping bent can be used (see Seed mixtures, pages 33–5.)

Wind

Because lawn grasses are so low growing, wind has very little effect on them and they certainly will not be damaged by a strong wind. However, from a practical point of view, an exposed windy site can make it a little more difficult to sow and establish a

Take factors such as light and shade into consideration when planning a lawn

lawn from seed. The soil will also dry out more quickly in a garden where there is a constant breeze. This can be an advantage insofar as the lawn will soon dry after rainfall, or a disadvantage, as the lawn may be more prone to drought in summer.

If establishing a lawn on a windy site, try to keep the seeded or turfed area constantly moist in order to aid establishment. On small areas that have been seeded, you can cover the area with garden fleece that has been pegged down to prevent it from blowing away. This will protect the seed and once the grass is 3–4cm (1½in) tall, the fleece cover can be removed.

Soil pH

A pH test measures the amount of calcium in the soil to determine whether the soil is acid or alkaline. Test kits are readily available from garden centres or DIY stores and only take a few minutes to use. The pH scale is from 1.0 to 14.0 with 7.0, the mid-point, being neutral. Any figure below this denotes acidity in the soil and above, alkalinity, caused by the higher amount of calcium present. The majority of garden soils fall between pH5.5 – 7.5. Generally speaking, finer grasses prefer a slightly acid soil and coarser grasses neutral to slightly alkaline, although a mid-way point is suitable for most grasses. Under normal circumstances you would not try to change the pH for a lawn, but knowing what it is in your garden gives you a little more background information.

Soil

Grass will grow in many different types of soil and you only have to look around the countryside to see farmers' fields full of lush grass growing in many different soils. If you have a reasonably well-structured, fertile soil you will be able to grow an excellent lawn. The species of grass that grow on each soil type do vary, however, with some preferring acid soils to alkaline and others moist soils to dry. The minimum depth of soil needed to grow a lawn is around 15cm (6in); much shallower, and the lawn would suffer in dry weather.

Soil types

Soil is made up of various different-sized mineral particles such as sand, silt and clay. A soil type is determined by the amount of each mineral. Added to the mineral content is organic matter in the form of animal and plant remains that have accumulated in the soil surface over many years.

If you were to make a cross section of the soil in your garden, it would comprise of different coloured layers. The upper layer, known as the topsoil, is usually the darkest in colour due to the organic matter it contains. This can vary in depth from 3–4cm (1½in) to half a metre (20in), is usually well-drained and is the layer where the grass roots will grow. Below the topsoil is the subsoil, which is often paler in colour and less open in structure; in some cases, this can cause drainage problems. The depth of the subsoil varies and can be shallow or deep. Below this level you will eventually find a rock or gravel layer.

Before preparing a site it is worth digging a hole in your garden to see what the soil profile looks like. If you suspect that the soil structure changes because of a slope or wet area at one end of the garden, dig a couple holes to check.

Sandy soils When handled, a sandy soil will feel gritty on your fingers and cannot be rolled into a shape. Individual sand particles are quite large, making a sandy soil open-textured and free-draining. The advantage of this is that you will be able to use the lawn shortly after it has rained as the water will have drained away. During the summer months, however, sandy soils can dry out very quickly and the lawn can suffer unless watered. Because water drains so quickly, nutrients and calcium are also washed through and as a result many sandy soils are naturally acid. These conditions are ideal for many of the fine-leaf grasses that are used on golf courses, such as fescues and bents.

It is a good idea to incorporate some organic matter such as garden compost or well-rotted manure into the area before the lawn is laid. This will help in the future with water and nutrient retention. Regular feeding will also be needed once the lawn is established, in order to keep the lawn in good condition.

Clay soils Clay particles are the smallest in size and stick together to form large clods of soil. When moist, clay soil can be moulded into a shape and it feels smooth and sticky. Due to the density of the clay particles, water drains much more slowly, and in heavy clay this can result in a

Problems with new sites

When dealing with a garden around a newly built property, you can sometimes come across problems caused by soil compaction and buried brick rubble. The soil may also be poor quality and very thin and patchy.

During the construction of a property, the topsoil is often removed and spread back until the job is completed. This layer of soil will conceal the compacted subsoil caused by diggers and dump trucks, and any waste bricks and cement. Alternatively, the builder may simply spread the subsoil dug out of the foundation on top of the better quality topsoil. Either method is likely to cause problems when you start to garden the plot. Ideally, if you are present while building is taking place, you should insist that all builders' waste is removed and that the subsoil is properly loosened before topsoil is added over the top.

What can be done if the problem remains? If you are faced with a difficult plot, deep digging over the entire plot is the best method to tackle the situation. Any brick rubble can be removed and used for paths and drains and any hard layers can be broken up. At the same time, add as much organic matter as possible.

On sites where poor quality subsoil has been spread over the better topsoil, the best approach is to have the poor soil scraped off and new topsoil brought in. This might seem a somewhat drastic measure, but in the long run it will be easier if you have done this than trying to improve the subsoil later on.

The crumbly, friable soil held in the left hand above will drain freely, unlike the stickier, smoother clay soil in the right hand, which retains water for longer periods

waterlogged lawn for many months of the year. As a result, some of the finer grasses may die out and coarser grasses take over. In situations where the soil is very wet and sticky, it is worth considering improving the soil and installing a basic drainage system (see Drainage, pages 22–4). To help improve clay soils, when cultivating work in some organic matter and gritty sand to open up the structure.

Although their poor drainage qualities can be a disadvantage, lawns growing on clay soils retain more nutrients and rarely dry out completely during the summer, which means the grass stays green for longer.

Loamy soils A loamy soil is a mixture of sand and clay particles in various proportions with added organic matter. The result is a crumbly soil that is both well-drained and at the same time retains moisture and nutrients. It will mould to a shape in your hand, but easily breaks down. If you are lucky enough to have such a soil you will have no difficulties preparing the site and establishing a lovely lawn!

Chalky soils Chalky soils tend to be very well-drained due to the chalk or limestone below, but the topsoil level is often shallow and in some situations barely deep enough to grow plants. When cultivating these shallow soils, care needs to be taken not to mix the topsoil with the stony subsoil. Lawns can usually be grown on chalky soils, although they may suffer in dry weather because of the rapid drainage properties.

Peaty soils Peat is formed by partially decayed plant remains which produce a dark, spongy soil that is very high in organic matter. Drainage can sometimes be a problem, especially in low-lying areas, and in most cases peaty soils are acidic. Certain types of grass are not suitable for these conditions, but as long as the soil is well cultivated and drained a lawn will grow without too many problems. Fescues and bents grow best on peaty acid soils. Some of the coarser-leaved grasses, such as Poa (meadow grasses) and Lolium (ryegrass)

One way to assess soil type is to dig several holes and pour water into them (see Tip)

can struggle in very acid soils, although modern varieties are much more tolerant of different conditions.

Drainage

On poorly drained soils, it is worth installing some type of drainage system before laying the lawn. Not only will the lawn benefit from the extra drainage but also surrounding plants and patio areas will be improved as a result of the removal of surplus water. In most cases the drainage system can be very simple and is mainly intended to take away slow-draining surface water.

Assessing drainage requirements

As part of assessing your garden, take note of what happens to yours or your neighbours' gardens after heavy rainfall. If puddles of water remain for a few days after rain, drainage is required. Digging a soil profile approximately 60cm (24in) deep will let you see what the subsoil is like and whether it is sandy or heavy clay. It will also identify any hard layers or pans that prevent water from draining. In some cases it is simply surface compaction that prevents water from seeping away, and once the area has been deeply forked over, water can once again drain freely.

Although the thought of establishing a lawn on wet, clay soil might be a little daunting, remember that grass is very tolerant and adaptable. A lawn is one of the best natural ways of drying out wet soils, and once the roots grow down into the soil as the lawn establishes, the whole plot will suddenly

TIP

Another worthwhile test is to dig a few small holes approximately 30cm (12in) deep in different places around the garden, then fill them with water. On sandy soils the water will drain quickly, whereas on clay soils it will take longer to go. If any water remains in the hole after approximately 12 hours, you should think about improving the drainage.

dry out. After rainfall the ground will drain faster, simply because the roots will have helped to open the heavy soil structure.

Where should the drain go? If you have identified a wet area in the garden where rain often stands after rainfall, for which additional drainage is required, the drain should be sited so that it passes through the wet area or as close as possible. If the whole area is wet, the drain can run down one side of the garden or diagonally across the garden.

French drains

This is a very simple method of draining surface water, especially where a paved area joins a lawn. A French drain is basically a trench that is filled with stones and gravel. In some cases it is covered over with a thin layer of soil and turf, or it may be left open with gravel on the top. If your garden is on a slight slope, the drain can follow the fall to remove water, or if there is an existing drainage ditch at the bottom of the garden it can run into it.

1 – Dig out a trench a minimum of 30cm (12in) deep and 25cm (10in) wide, making sure that the base of the trench has a gentle slope to carry the water away.

2 – Fill the base of the hole with brick rubble or large stones and then fill to the top of the trench with smaller gravel, roughly 12mm (½in) in diameter.

A French drain is easy to construct and extremely effective

1

2

Land drains

Where something more substantial is needed to remove surface water, a land drain can be installed that runs into a ditch or soakaway. To create a soakaway, dig a hole at least 1m (3ft) deep and square and fill it with broken bricks, rubble and gravel. Surface water is piped to the hole where it can slowly soak through the subsoil. When installing a land drain, a single drain may be sufficient to remove the water, or you may wish to run a couple of short side drains into the main one.

This type of drainage system is sometimes referred to as a 'herring-bone drain' because of the nature of the design. The main central drain has several lateral drains running into it at angles.

Traditionally, clay pipes were used but pipes are now made from perforated plastic that allow water through. When installing a land drain, check the ground levels to make sure there is a fall on the pipe to carry the water way. The gradient only needs to be slight; around 1:100 is sufficient and this can be checked with a surveyor's level.

For areas where you intend to install a drainage system there are specialist contractors who will undertake the work, or if you wish to carry it out yourself, trench digging machines can be hired.

1 – Dig a trench approximately 45–60cm (18–24in) deep and 25cm (10in) wide, with a slight, even fall. Keep the topsoil separate and dispose of the subsoil.

2 – Add a thin layer of gravel to the base of the trench.

3 – Lay a perforated plastic drainage pipe on top of the stones; these can be bought from a builder's yard.

4 – Cover over the pipe with more gravel and then use a strip of porous landscape fabric on top of the gravel. This is to prevent soil washing down into the drain. Finish off by topping up the trench with roughly 25cm (10in) of topsoil, lightly firming as you go to prevent settlement one the lawn is laid.

1

2

3

4

Preparing for a New Lawn

Once laid and established, a lawn usually remains in the garden for many years; indeed, many of the sweeping lawns around country houses are centuries old. With this in mind, it is vital to prepare the ground thoroughly before you consider laying turf or sowing seed. Grass will grow in most situations, and if you were to simply scatter some seed on a piece of bare earth it would probably grow and be green. However, it would not produce a quality lawn, and very quickly you would begin to get problems with compaction, weeds and mosses. Trying to improve a lawn that is in poor condition due to the fact that the ground was not prepared properly in the first place is much more difficult than the soil preparation itself.

Weed control

To allow you to be able to prepare the lawn surface, the ground needs to be cleared and weed free. The degree of work involved here will depend on how poor the site is to start with. Large objects such as bricks, pieces of wood or old garden waste should be disposed of before you start to control the weed population.

On overgrown sites where there is a large population of established perennial weeds, such as stinging nettles, docks and willow herb, it may take several months to get the weeds under control. The more thorough you are in removing the weeds the easier you will find it to complete the final soil preparations. Clearing an overgrown site one day and laying a lawn the next can be done, and often is by some contractors, but it is not the best way to produce a good quality lawn.

In areas where mainly annual weeds are growing, such as chickweed and groundsel, ground preparation can be done much faster as these weeds are easier to control.

Using a chemical weedkiller

One of the best ways of controlling all types of weeds, but especially perennials ones, is to use a weedkiller. Glyphosate is the chemical that is most widely available and can be found as the active ingredient on many branded products. When used as per the instructions on the container it is very effective and safe enough that children and pets need not be excluded from treated areas once the spray has dried on the weed leaf. It works by being absorbed through the leaves into the plant, killing all parts including the roots. This process can take up to three weeks on some weeds, so you do need to be patient. In some cases where perennial weeds are well established, it may be necessary to spray the weeds more than once if you find they start to grow again from the roots. Be careful when using glyphosate, as it will kill all plants, not just weeds, and should only be directed onto weeds and unwanted plants.

Once the weeds have died down they can be raked off or forked out and the soil and the ground prepared in readiness for the lawn. Glyphosate does not remain in the soil and will not affect the new lawn.

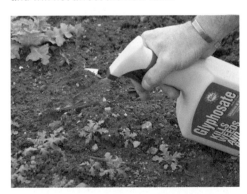

Glyphosate is an effective weedkiller but must be directed carefully, as it will kill all plants

TIP

The best time to use glyphosate is when the weeds are actively growing and have a good leaf cover during spring and summer. Do not be tempted to spray with this chemical mixture when the tips of weeds are pushing through the soil, as the small leaf area will not be able to absorb enough of the chemical to kill a large root. That said, most weedkillers work better on new growth, so it is a good idea to cut down tall perennial weeds and spray the re-growth when it is approximately 15–20cm (6–8in) tall in order to achieve the best results.

Hoeing needs to be undertaken regularly in order to be an effective form of weed control

There are also several organic weedkillers available based on natural fatty acids. These work very quickly by scorching off the stems and foliage of the weeds.

Non-chemical weed control

If you do not wish to use a weedkiller, it is possible to control the weeds in other ways. These methods are effective but may take a little longer.

Digging out One way is to dig out all perennial weeds with a garden fork. Care needs to be taken to remove all pieces of the roots, as any left in the ground will inevitably

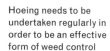

Annual and perennial weeds must be removed from lawns on a regular basis if they are to be prevented from swamping plants. Use a hoe or pull them out by hand

re-grow. This can be done at any time of the year and may need repeating if new weeds appear. Although this method is a little more strenuous in the first instance, in the process of digging you are also loosening the soil and breaking up any surface compaction, as well as removing the weeds.

Hoeing Using a push hoe can be very effective at controlling the seedlings of annual weeds. Although annual weeds are not normally a problem in an established lawn or when turf is being laid, they can be a nuisance on spring-seeded lawns. Where there is a large quantity of weed seeds in the soil, the weeds can smother a newly sown lawn. To reduce the amount of weed seeds, leave the ground fallow for a season and as the weeds germinate, hoe them off every few weeks. If you do this over a season the weed seed population will be vastly reduced.

Rotavating This is another method of controlling annual weeds which involves using a special rotavator tool. If rotavating is undertaken regularly, the procedure gets rid of the weeds by simply chopping them up and burying them. Where perennial weeds are a problem they should be dealt with first, as otherwise the rotavating will chop the roots into many pieces and spread the plants (see Rotavating, page 30).

Scorching A small flame gun is also an effective way of dealing with annual weeds. These can be bought from DIY stores or hired for a weekend. The idea is not to burn off the weed, just simply scorch the leaves, which will result in the plant withering and dying in a day or two.

Direct the flame right onto the head of the offending weed

Smothering Black polythene or old carpet laid over the weeds will block out light and smother them. In the case of perennial weeds, the cover will need to be left in place for several months, but annual weeds will be killed in two weeks. This method is ideal if you have time on your hands and are planning a lawn for several months ahead. When using any form of ground cover material to smother weeds, make sure it is securely anchored down with wood or bricks.

Levelling the site

A lawn certainly does not have to be perfectly level – and in the majority of cases the lawn can follow the natural contours of the garden – but it does need to be level enough to mow. Gentle undulations are fine for a mower, but if the land has lots of humps and hollows, mowing will be very difficult and the tops of the humps may be scalped as the mower passes over.

Raking

Very often the levelling can be done by eye, so that once you have dug over and improved the soil it can simply be raked over several times to get the desired finish. This method of levelling is perfectly adequate as long as there is a good depth of topsoil. If the topsoil is shallow, when the high spots are raked into the low spots you will finish up with some areas of the lawn where the soil will be too thin. This will result in a patchy lawn and uneven growth. As you level the soil, if you are having to move more than 7.5cm (3in) of topsoil, it is worth considering buying some good quality topsoil to build up the level so that all areas of the lawn have a reasonable thickness.

TIP When adding new topsoil to build up levels, spread the soil over the entire area and mix it into the existing soil a little to prevent different layers of soil forming. Bags of topsoil are available from garden centres if you only need a small amount, but for larger quantities it is best to buy in bulk bags or lorry loads from garden centres or specialist turf suppliers.

Levelling with pegs

If you wish to have a completely level lawn in all directions it can be achieved by the use of a series of wooden pegs driven into the ground. A path or driveway can be used as a datum point from where the level is taken. The pegs are normally knocked into the ground to form a grid system, with the top of the peg being the finished level. Alternatively, a line can be drawn 2.5cm (1in) down from the top of the peg with white paint. The white line becomes the finished level but leaves some of the peg visible above ground level, which makes them much easier to see. A straight edge or string line

Dealing with a sloping lawn

Where the lawn slopes – either gently or steeply – but you still want to achieve a flat, even surface, pegs and a string line can be used. Knock in two pegs, one at the top of the slope and the other at the bottom. Stretch a strong garden line between the two pegs and fasten the line to them. It needs to be really tight to prevent any sag in the string. This forms the line of the slope; you can then knock in more pegs to the string level, so that the lawn will be even from top to bottom. Across the slope you can carry on using a tight string line or a straight edge and spirit level across the pegs.

1

2

3

can then be used between the pegs to established the final soil level of the lawn.

1 – Position and knock in pegs across the lawn area to form a grid spacing them approximately 1m (1yd) apart. Lay a straight edge from one peg to another and check the level with a spirit level, adjusting the pegs as you go.

2 – Shovel the soil between the pegs to establish a level surface. Alternatively, a little new soil can be added to reach the tops of the pegs.

3 – Rake the soil level between the pegs either by eye, or by drawing a wooden board across the pegs to grade out the soil; this job is best done by two people, one on each end of the board. When you are happy with the level, remember to remove all of the pegs, as if left in the soil they will rot and encourage fungi to grow. They will also hinder lawn maintenance in the future.

Subsoil levelling

If the topsoil in your garden is not very deep and it is impractical to import new soil, you will need to adopt a different levelling technique on bumpy sites. First, remove the topsoil from the lawn area and store it to the side. Then dig over and rotavate the subsoil to loosen it, before raking it level. After raking, tread over the whole area in order to firm it and so prevent settlement at a later date. The topsoil can then be spread back over the levelled area to a uniform depth.

This type of levelling is a little more drastic and not the sort of thing you would want to do on a large area, but for a small lawn it is worth doing as a last resort. If this type of levelling needs to be done on a large area, a mechanical digger can be used. If the subsoil is clay the task becomes a little more difficult, but it can still be done.

> **TIP**
> When using pegs to establish a level, note how many you use. You will then know if they have all been removed afterwards.

Cultivating the Soil

When the ground has been cleared of weeds and surface debris you can start cultivating the soil, which involves turning the soil over and loosening the surface either by digging or rotavating the area. The way this is done will depend on the size of the plot and the type of soil. Although grass will grow quite satisfactorily in soil that is between 15–20cm (6–8in) deep, it is beneficial to cultivate the soil as deep as possible. During cultivations, remove any buried rubble and dig out any roots from old trees and shrubs, as if they are left to decay naturally below the soil you are likely to have problems with toadstools and fungi in the lawn in years to come.

Digging

For small plots, digging by hand is often the best way of cultivating the soil and it saves having to borrow or hire a rotavator. However,

TIP

When digging with a spade always keep your back straight and bend your knees to avoid back strain. Do not attempt too much in one go: digging little and often is the best way. In addition to digging, you may also find it useful to turn the soil over with a garden fork to break down any larger lumps of soil.

digging is very physical and can be extremely hard work, so be realistic and make sure that you are up to the whole task before you pick up your fork and spade.

Dig over the plot to the depth of the spade, which is roughly 22.5cm (9in) deep. This is known as single digging and is usually all that is required for light, sandy soils. If the soil is heavy clay it is also well worth the effort of double digging to improve drainage (see page 30), although this may not be an option if there is only a thin layer of topsoil above a solid clay subsoil; you should never mix topsoil with subsoil. You may also want to install some form of drainage to the area (see Drainage, pages 22–4).

Digging is easiest if you begin by breaking up the soil with a fork before using your spade

Adding organic matter

At the same time as you dig over the soil, it is a good idea to incorporate some organic matter, such as compost or well-rotted manure. This will help to replenish nutrients, open up the structure of clay soil and increase the moisture-holding capacity of lighter sandy soils. Although organic matter will improve the soil, do not apply large amounts, as when it rots down the soil will settle and the lawn can become uneven.

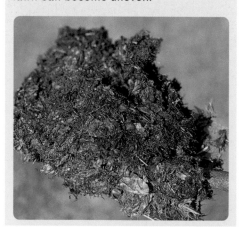

Rotavating

On areas that are too large to dig by hand, a mechanical rotavator or cultivator can be used. These can be hired from tool shops or bought from garden centres and DIY stores. Various designs of these machines are available, but all have rotating steel blades that turn the soil over.

Rotavators can be used on all soil types, but loamy and sandy soils are particularly easy to rotavate due to their looser, more friable structure. By crossing the area you wish to cultivate in two or three directions, you can create a neat finish to an even depth in relatively little time. Make sure that you rotavate to the same depth across the whole site: if you rotavate some areas much deeper than others, not only is there a chance that the grass will grow unevenly, but the ground may settle at different levels once the lawn is laid. This is not only unsightly, it can be inconvenient if not dangerous, depending on what the lawn is used for.

Avoid digging or rotavating when the soil is very wet as this damages the open structure of the soil, plus it is far more difficult to work the rotavator.

Double digging There are various methods of double digging, but for a lawn all you need to do is follow this simple method.

1 – First dig a trench the width and depth of the spade at one end of the plot, leaving the excavated soil to one side.

2 – Fork over the base of this trench and then dig another trench, turning the soil from this second trench to fill the first.

3 – Carry on turning over the soil and forking the base of each trench until you reach the end of the plot.

4 – When you have finished digging the plot, fill the final trench with the soil from the original trench.

1

2

3

4

A rotavator is often the easiest option, if your soil is heavy or digging is physically beyond you

Dealing with a soil pan

In heavy soil, as the blade of the rotavator slices through the clay it can smear to create a hard layer – or pan – a short distance down. This can impede drainage. Pans tend to be more of a problem on land that has been cultivated on a regular basis to the same depth for a long period. If you suspect this problem, rotavate a small area and dig a hole to see if a hard layer can be found. If a definite layer is found, try to rotavate deeper than the pan to break it up, or push a garden fork into the soil and lever it back to raise and loosen the soil.

Final preparations

After levelling and cultivating the site you can start to carry out the final preparations for laying your new lawn. It is often thought that the final soil surface needs to be better if you are creating the lawn from seed, but in fact it is the same whether you are making the lawn from seed or turf. Ultimately, your lawn will only be as good as your preparations.

Raking and treading

Although the previously described cultivations have been undertaken primarily in order to loosen the soil, when the soil is finally prepared, you will need a firm seed-bed or planting surface. If the surface is too soft, the lawn will eventually settle and become uneven; if the soil is too compacted, it will be difficult for the roots of the grass to penetrate into it and drainage may be impeded, causing pools of water to form on the surface of the lawn.

Prepare the soil surface through a process of thorough treading and raking. Treading firms the soil evenly and breaks down any lumps of soil, and the raking helps to form a crumbly surface or 'tilth' which is ideal for the grass seed to grow into. The amount of raking and treading required will depend on the soil type, and it may be necessary to tread the soil over two or three times in different directions. However, it really is worth spending a little time getting this part right, as the final level you produce will be the finished level of your new lawn.

TIP

When raking the area, if you find soil sticks to the bottom of your boots, the soil is too wet to work on. Leave it for a day and try again.

To carry out this process you only need a garden rake and your feet, and perhaps the help of someone else with large feet, especially if the lawn area is big. Some people use a roller instead of treading the soil, and certainly on a large area it is much faster. The disadvantage of a roller is it does not firm the soil as evenly as when done by foot. The roller will tend to ride over any hard areas and sink in the soft spots, so should only be used as a last resort. If you do use a roller, it should weigh less than 150kg (3cwt).

1

2

3

1 – Once the soil has been cultivated, rake over the surface to establish a rough level and remove any large stones that have been brought to the surface. There is no need to remove every stone, as these are needed for the natural drainage of the soil, but it is a good idea to remove anything larger than 2.5cm (1in) in diameter, which might impede the growth of the grass seed.

2 – Firm the soil with your feet by putting your weight on your heels and then using a shuffling motion to work your way up and down the area. Ensure that all parts of the planting surface are properly firmed.

3 – Rake the soil over once again to produce a fine tilth, digging the tines of the rake into the soil no more than 2.5cm (1in). This process should be repeated at right angles for the final finish.

When finished, the seed bed should be fine and firm. A good test as to the firmness of the bed is to walk on the area. Ideally, you should leave a shallow footprint. If you sink, the soil is too soft and if you leave no footprint it is too hard, and more work will be required.

Applying fertilizer

Although there will already be nutrients in the soil, it is a good idea to add some extra ones in order to help the new grass establish. Ideally, this should be applied a few days before the seed is sown or the turf is laid. This gives the fertilizer time to start and release the nutrients into the soil. In practice, this is not always possible. If the lawn is going to be laid as soon as the soil has been prepared, then the time to apply the fertilizer is when the soil is being given its final rake over.

The fertilizer should contain the three main nutrients that plants need, (N) nitrogen, (P) phosphorus and (K) potassium. These will supply the essential nutrients required for healthy growth and establishment. The phosphorus is especially important for new lawns, as it encourages root growth.

Some seed companies sell a pre-seed fertilizer that has the correct nutrient balance and this is suitable not only for seeded lawns but also for turf. If this is not available, any general fertilizer can be used. These tend to contain a balance of nutrients that will promote root and grass growth. When using a specialist fertilizer, always follow the instructions on the packet or apply a general fertilizer at a rate of 150–200g/sq m (4–6oz/sq yd), lightly raked into the soil surface.

Growing from Seed

The main advantage of growing a lawn from seed is that you can choose exactly what type of grass you want to suit the needs of your garden. Seed companies now supply a wide range of different lawn seed mixes for every situation. A lawn is also considerably cheaper to establish when it is grown from seed, and this is well worth taking into account if you are grassing down a large area. The disadvantage of using seed is that you will have to wait a little longer for the lawn to establish compared with a turf lawn.

Buying Seed

It is very important that you buy good quality seed from a reputable supplier. The seed you sow over the prepared area will form a lawn for many years to come, and if it is poor quality or the wrong type, very often the only solution is to dig it up and start again.

Most seed companies use seed varieties that have been developed and tested for sports and amenity uses and will often display this on the packet. These perform superbly in a garden situation and are much dwarfer in habit and uniform in growth than agricultural types. The seed companies may

also state the percentage of each type of grass seed used in the mixture and sometimes the individual cultivars (cultivated varieties) used. However, new cultivars are being developed all the time, so it is more common for suppliers to list only the general grass types in order to avoid confusion.

Many seed companies also treat their lawn seed with an additive such as seaweed extract. This aids fast germination and establishment by supplying valuable minerals and encouraging beneficial bacteria in the soil.

Understanding Seed Mixtures

The range of seed mixtures on sale means that you can establish a lawn in all situations. Even in a single garden you may find it necessary to use more than one seed mixture to accommodate your needs. For example, you would need a hardwearing mixture for a lawn where children will play, whereas for an area under trees you would need a different mixture. Each specific mixture will contain a selection of grasses that grow best in each situation.

Hardwearing

This mix will predominantly contain dwarf ryegrass and a small percentage of creeping red fescue. It is a popular type of mix and the sort you would expect to find on a sports field. Its hardwearing qualities and speed of establishment and recovery make it ideal for a lawn where children and pets use it frequently or for paths between beds and borders. Seed companies will each have their own brand name for this mixture, such as 'Tuffgrass', 'Family lawn' or 'Amenity mix'. The dwarf varieties of ryegrass used mean the lawn will withstand regular mowing down to approximately 12mm (½in). Cutting with a rotary mower is usual, but you could use a cylinder mower.

Beware the 'Wonder Grass'

Always avoid cheap grass seed that gives no indication of the seed mix. Sometimes grass seed is advertized as being very fast to grow and establish, creating a beautiful lawn in no time at all – a type of 'Wonder Grass'. These mixes may well grow and establish quickly – the reason is because agricultural grass varieties have been used instead of garden varieties. Agricultural grass needs to grow quickly for grazing and hay making purposes, and the seed is also much cheaper. The result will be a very fast and vigorous growing lawn, but one made up of coarse grasses that will not stand close mowing.

Fine lawn

This seed mixture is designed for creating a fine-quality lawn and comprises a selection of creeping red fescue, chewings fescue and browntop bent, but no ryegrass. When established the lawn will have a very fine appearance and is ideal for a formal lawn. Due to the absence of ryegrass, the lawn will not be as hardwearing as a family-type lawn, although the modern cultivars of fescue and bent are moderately wear resistant. To maintain the fine look to the lawn it is best mown fairly closely, to 5mm (⅕in) for a bowling green quality, but 10mm (⅓in) is more usual, using a cylinder mower (see Mowing, pages 49–52).

General purpose

For a lawn that falls mid-way between a hardwearing lawn and a fine lawn, many seed companies produce a general mix that contains ryegrass, fescues and bents. This produces a lawn that has a good appearance and is also tough and hardwearing. This all round mixture is perfect for a quality lawn in a domestic situation. Mowing can be done with either a cylinder or rotary mower, and the grasses included will withstand mowing down to approximately 12mm (½in).

Shady lawns

The introduction of seed mixtures that will grow in shady places has made creating a lawn in these challenging circumstances much easier for the home gardener. Where an area was once sparse, thin grass, you can now establish a decent sward. Shade in a garden can be caused by trees, walls or tall buildings, and in this situation some grasses

find it difficult to establish. In a shade mixture a selection of fescues, bents and meadow grass cultivars are used because of their ability to grow in poor light conditions. These grasses are also tolerant of dry soil conditions, which are often a problem in shade, especially under trees. Although the grasses used can withstand close mowing, when grown in shady conditions it is better to allow them to grow a little longer and maintain the sward at around 25mm (1in) in height, cutting usually with a rotary mower, although you can use a cylinder mower if it is set high. If mown too closely in a shady area, grass takes longer to recover and regrow.

Wildflower meadows

Lawns that contain wildflowers are becoming more and more popular and several seed companies offer wildflower or meadow mixtures. These contain a selection of grasses and perennial wild flowers such as knapweed, ox-eye daisy, clover, bird's-foot trefoil, cowslip, buttercups and many others. They are ideal for attracting insects into the garden and for creating a natural area, but a meadow is not like a traditional lawn that is mown regularly. Perennial wildflowers can be slow to germinate and establish and it can be several years before you get a good balance of grass and flowers (see Other Lawn Features – Wildflowers in the Lawn, pages 95–9).

Seed Mixtures and their Applications

Seed mix	Properties	Use	Mowing
Hardwearing	quick to establish and recover; withstands heavy traffic	activities lawn; paths between beds and borders	to 12mm (½in), with rotary or cylinder mower
Fine lawn	fine appearance; low to moderate wear resistance	formal lawn	to min. 5mm (⅕in) but usually 10mm (⅓in) with cylinder mower
General purpose	good looking; relatively hardwearing	quality family lawn	to 12mm (½in) with rotary or cylinder mower
Shady	will tolerate shady, dry conditions	sowing under trees, next to walls and other shady situations	to 25mm (1in) with rotary mower
Drought tolerant	will tolerate dry conditions	sowing in well-drained areas	to 12mm (½in) with rotary mower
Low maintenance	slow growing for less frequent mowing	sowing in inaccessible areas; for ease	to 25mm (1in) with rotary mower

Drought tolerant

For areas where the soil is very well drained and dries out during the summer, or where it is difficult to irrigate, a mixture of grasses that are drought tolerant can be used. The selection of grasses is similar to those used in a shade mix – fescues, bents and meadow grass – although they are blended in different proportions. The grasses have a fine leaf and will tolerate fairly close mowing to 12mm (½in), although in dry weather it is advisable to allow the lawn to grow a little longer. Mow with a rotary mower or cylinder mower set high.

Low maintenance

A low maintenance mixture contains grasses such as fine-leaved dwarf ryegrass, creeping red fescue and bent grass. The cultivars that have been chosen are slow growing and dwarf in habit. The main advantage is that the grass will need mowing less frequently, making them ideal for areas where mowing is difficult or you want to save time. Although a low maintenance mixture will make a reasonably good looking lawn, it will not be as fine as some of the other mixtures available. The ryegrass content, however, will give durability to the lawn. Mowing is usually down to 20mm (¾in), usually with a rotary mower or cylinder mower set high.

TIP

Grass seed can be stored for approximately two years in a cool dry place, but after that the viability will quickly reduce.

When to sow

The two main times for sowing grass seed are spring and autumn. Sowing can be done at other times, but in spring and autumn when the soil is warm and moist the seed will quickly establish. Depending on the local weather conditions, seed should germinate between 14–21 days after sowing, although treated seed may germinate a little faster in some areas.

If seed is sown during the summer months, you will need to water the soil in order to keep it moist.

Spring sowing

Seed sown in spring will germinate and grow away very quickly. The aim is to establish the young grass before the heat and dry weather of summer. However, if you sow too early in spring the ground is likely to be too cold and wet for the grass seed to germinate effectively. Grass sown late in the spring, on the other hand, may suffer during its first summer from drought unless water is on hand to irrigate. Annual weeds can also be a problem in spring and will compete with the seedling grass.

When to sow The best time to sow is mid-spring when the days start to get a little longer and warmer. In good growing conditions, a lawn sown in mid-spring will be established enough to use by mid-summer.

Autumn sowing

The main advantage of sowing in the autumn is that the lawn will have all winter and spring to establish a good root system before the lawn is used. Annual weeds are much less of a problem in the autumn and cause very little competition for the grass.

Although very little leaf growth will be made during the winter months, the roots will continue to develop and come spring the grass will grow away very quickly and be less prone to drought than a spring sown lawn.

When to sow The best time to sow is early autumn while the soil is still warm but after it has been moistened by the first rains. An autumn sown lawn will be established enough to use by the following late spring.

TIP Before sowing, shake the seed packet to mix the seeds thoroughly together, as otherwise the small seeds will settle to the bottom and will be sown last. Try to save a small amount of seed for any areas where the grass does not germinate very well, or for any damage that occurs later on.

How to Sow

Seed can be sown by hand or by a spreader and the method you use will depend on the size of the lawn. Small irregular shaped lawns are best sown by hand, but for a very large open area a spreader will speed things up.

Sowing rates

Sowing rates are usually quoted in grams per square metre (g/sq m) or ounces per square yard (oz/sq yd) and will vary slightly depending on the type of grass that you are sowing. Coarser grasses such as ryegrass produce larger seeds than fescues or bents and therefore to get the same amount of seeds per given area you need to sow a larger weight. Traditionally mixtures containing ryegrass are sown at 45g/sq m (1½oz/sq yd) and mixtures without ryegrass at 28g/sq m (1oz/sq yd). Most seed companies opt for a mid-way sowing rate of 35g/sq m (1¼oz/sq yd) to make life simpler for the user. The rates are only approximate and if the seed is sown a little thinner or thicker it will not make too much difference, but try not to deviate too much from the recommended coverage. General advice is:

Calculating seed quantities

To calculate the amount of seed you need, measure the length and width of your plot to find the area. Multiply this by the sowing rate to give you the amount of seed required.

Example

Size of plot:	6.75m x 4.25m = 28.68sq m
Sowing rate:	35g/sq m
Seed quantity:	28.68 x 35 = 1,003g (approx. 1kg)

Note: Work in either metric or imperial, rather than trying to convert.

- If seed is sown very thinly, it will take much longer for the lawn to establish and weeds will invade the lawn quickly.
- If seed is sown very thickly, there are likely to be problems with fungal diseases in the young lawn caused by overcrowding.

Sowing by hand

If you have not sown grass seed before, it is a good idea to mark out a small area with four canes to create a square metre or yard. Then weigh and sow the correct amount of seed in the square. This will show you what the sowing density looks like on the ground so that you can replicate it for the rest of the lawn area. You can then sow the grass seed over the prepared area scattering the seed by hand.

Sowing by spreader

For large areas a fertilizer spreader with a spinning plate can be used. The seed in the hopper drops through an adjustable hole onto a plate that spins when the spreader is pushed forward. The faster you walk the further the seed is spread, making this type

A spreader is ideal for large areas, but not smaller ones, as seed might be scattered into adjacent borders

A gentle raking over will allow the seed to make proper contact with the soil and become established

of spreader perfect for large areas. Calibrating the sowing rate is a little more difficult with this type of spreader.

As an alternative to a spinning spreader, you can use a drop spreader that spreads the seed the width of the machine. The seed falls through a series of holes as you walk forward. This type of spreader is much more controllable and you can calibrate the seed rate by testing an area on a sheet of polythene before hand.

Raking and watering in

Once the seed has been evenly sown across the entire planting area, it should be lightly raked into the soil surface. This is not done to completely bury the seed, but it does help to keep the seed in contact with moist soil. It also removes footprints and wheel marks

Mark out the first square metre (yard) of the sowing area to gauge visually how much seed will be needed

if a spreader was used to distribute the seed. If the soil is moist, there is nothing else to do until the seeds germinate. If the soil is dry, use a fine sprinkler to lightly water the soil, taking care not to disturb or wash away the seed. In good conditions, generally the first sign of green shoots should be seen in two to three weeks.

Aftercare of a Seeded Lawn

When lawns are sown in spring or autumn the soil is usually moist enough for the seed to germinate without watering. If, however, the weather remains dry for two weeks after sowing, it is worth watering the areas with a gentle spray. Usually the first signs of new grass will be seen after a couple of weeks, depending on the soil temperature. Allow the seedling grass to establish until it is around 5cm (2in) tall before carrying out other work.

Stone picking Choose a dry day when the soil is not too wet and walk over the area to pick off any stones that have worked their way to the surface. If left they may be caught by the mower.

Remove all stones that might damage the mower or impede growth

Rolling If you have a small garden roller or are able to borrow one, the grass can be

given a light rolling, although this is not essential. The rolling will push any small stones into the soil surface and will bend over the blades of grass. This makes the grass 'tiller' (produce new shoots from the base of the plant).

First cut The first cut also makes the grass 'tiller'. You just want to take the top off the grass and for that a rotary mower with the blades set high is ideal. Either collect the clippings in the mower box or carefully rake them away. If the mower has a roller on it you can roll and cut in one operation. Over

Rolling can be beneficial in encouraging growth in new lawns, but it is not an essential measure to take

When you make the first cut of a newly established lawn, be careful not to cut too close

the next two or three cuts, the height of cut can gradually be lowered until you are cutting at the desired height.

Watering Until the new lawn is established it may be necessary to water the grass in periods of dry weather. Grass seed sown in the autumn is less likely to need watering than a spring sown one. The aim is to keep the soil moist until the grass has made some deeper roots, when it will be able to fend for itself.

Weeding and feeding On any seeded area some weeds will grow, but providing the ground preparation was done correctly, they should be mainly annual weeds that have grown from dormant seed in the soil. These annual weeds will die out after the lawn has been mown several times. Any perennial weeds can be removed by hand before they become too established.

> **TIP** Lawn weedkillers should not be used on new lawns until they are at least six months old, otherwise the young grasses may be damaged. For the first feed use only fertilizer, not a combined weed and feed.

If you used a pre-seed fertilizer prior to sowing the grass, it will not need any extra feed for several months. An autumn sown lawn can be fed for the first time the following mid- to late spring and a spring sown lawn can be fed in mid-summer.

One of the main reasons for feeding a seedling lawn sparingly for the first few months is to prevent the soft young grasses being attacked by diseases such as 'damping off' (see Pests & Diseases, pages 136–40). This is a fungal disease that can attack seedlings while they are still establishing and it is often worse in damp conditions or when the grass growth is crowded or lush. By holding back on the feed until the grass is more established you will be lessening the chances of the lawn being attacked.

Even on new lawns that look to be heavily infested with seedling or perennial weeds, regular mowing over a period of a few months will mow out the majority of the weeds, thicken the grass cover and totally transform the appearance of the lawn.

Hand weed or dig out annual and perennial weeds with a trowel, disturbing the lawn as little as possible

Laying Turf

Making a lawn from turf creates an instant effect, although it needs a few weeks to establish before it can be used. The ground preparation is the same as for a seed-based lawn, but rather than having to wait for seed to grow, the pieces of turf can be laid very quickly to transform brown earth into a lush green lawn. Where you want instant effect and a lawn that can be used reasonably soon after laying for children and pets to play on, turf is without doubt the best choice.

Your turves will most likely be delivered rolled up like carpets

Buying Turf

There are various grades of turf readily available to suit the type of lawn that you are trying to create. Suppliers can be found in telephone directories, the classified section of local newspapers, gardening magazines and garden centres. It is worth considering the following advice to ensure that you get your money's worth:

• Where possible ask to see a sample of the turf before buying – this should not be a problem if you are buying from a garden centre that is a stockist for a turf company, as they will have regular deliveries.
• Try to get the recommendation of a supplier from a friend or neighbour who has ordered some turf in the past.
• Contact several turf suppliers to compare prices and to check how the turf is sold. Some companies still sell by the yard, whereas others sell by the metre. You also need to ask about delivery charges and whether the price is inclusive of VAT.

Types of Turf
Meadow turf

This is the lowest grade of turf that you are likely to find and the cheapest. It is basically a farmer's grass field that has been used for grazing cattle or sheep. The turf company

will rent the field for a season and mow the grass several times before lifting the turf. If broad-leaved weeds are present in large numbers, the turf contractor will usually spray the turf with a selective weed killer to control them.

These grasses are usually on the coarse side but with regular mowing, feeding and maintenance you can establish a fairly good sward that is hardwearing. When buying this type of turf you have to be prepared for some unevenness in the thickness of the turf, a few weeds and possibly some natural fertilizer in the form of animal manure! Meadow turf is often cut slightly thicker than cultivated turf to hold the roots together and this adds to the weight. Meadow turf is ideal for where you want to create a large area of lawn as in-expensively as possible.

Cultivated turf

Cultivated turf is grass that is grown especially for making lawns or sports fields. Large areas of land are cultivated and seeded by contractors in order to produce

TIP

If you are creating two lawns from scratch, one at the front of the property and one at the rear, to save money you might want to make one lawn from turf and grow the other from seed. Lay the lawn you will get most use out of with turf so that you can enjoy it soonest. Or it may be that one lawn area is more difficult to access and therefore easier to raise from seed than trying to move the turves around.

the turf, which is maintained to a high standard prior to lifting.

There are several grades of cultivated turf available, from very fine grass mixtures used for golf greens and bowling greens, to hardwearing ryegrass mixes for football pitches. For domestic lawns the choice is usually between a mixture which comes either with or without ryegrass. The turf is cut to an even thickness, is lighter to handle, weed free and has a dense sward.

The larger growers of cultivated turf tend to be members of an association that will have strict guidelines that the grower must adhere to, ensuring a consistent and high quality product. The size of the rolls of turf varies from supplier to supplier, although most produce a roll that equates to 1sq m (1sq yd). Some suppliers also cut large rolls of up to 25sq m (25sq yd) that have to be laid by a special machine.

Cultivated turf is a very high quality turf grown using all lawn varieties rather than strong growing agricultural grasses – it is the most popular type of turf available.

Flotation turf

This is another type of cultivated turf that is not yet as widely available as field grown cultivated turf. A thin compost layer and plastic reinforcing net is laid over a polythene membrane and seeded with the grass mixture. The whole area is irrigated to keep the compost moist, which in turn encourages rapid establishment of the grass. Because the polythene prevents the roots from growing downwards, a dense matt of roots is produced very quickly that holds the turf together. In excellent growing conditions the process from seeding to harvesting the turf can take as little as several weeks.

Lifting the turf is simply a case of cutting to size and rolling it up like a carpet. Because there is no root disturbance when the turf is lifted, once laid onto prepared ground the new turf will grow and establish very quickly indeed. Flotation turf is also lighter in weight than other types of turf, which can be an advantage. The cost of flotation turf is on a par with the best quality cultivated turf.

When to Lay

Turf can be laid at most times of the year, although spring and autumn are the best times when the soil is moist and warm. Turf can be laid through the summer and winter, but avoid drought conditions and periods when the soil is waterlogged or frozen. By laying the lawn in spring or autumn, the grass will root into the soil and establish much faster.

In spring or autumn, there is also less need for irrigation than in summer and in the winter grass can be slow to root because of the cold soil. However, turf is very tough and as long as it is laid properly, you can create a new lawn almost any time.

The greens of golf courses are created from the best turf or seed

TIP

If you are turfing an area that is difficult to get water to, avoid laying the turf from mid-spring onwards. The best time to do the work is from mid-autumn to early spring when the ground is naturally moist and the conditions are cooler.

Laying Turf

Laying turf is a very simple process, and as long as you have carefully prepared the area, putting the turf down is the easy part.

Before starting to lay the turf, make sure that you have got all the tools and equipment to hand that you are likely to need. These will include:

- a rake – to do any last minute preparations
- a half-moon edging iron – for cutting the turf
- a string line – if you want to create a straight edge
- a wheelbarrow – for carrying and moving the turf around.

1 – Where possible, start by laying a row of turf around the perimeter of the lawn using a path or string line as a guide. This forms a solid edge to the lawn and is much better than an edge made of small pieces of turf. If the area to be turfed abuts a straight edge that is already in place, as shown in the sequence opposite, so much the better.

2 – Where pieces of turf join, make sure that the ends are tightly butted together. Avoid leaving any edges exposed or gaps between the turf, as weeds will establish quickly if allowed to squeeze up between the turves.

3 – To prevent damaging the newly laid turf, work from a wooden board, moving it forward with each row. This will spread your weight and also help to firm the turf down as you work across the area.

4 – When you come to the end of a row, cut off any spare turf with a half-moon edging iron and use this off-cut piece to begin the next row. This minimizes waste and also helps to keep the joints staggered.

5 – Once all the turf is laid and any gaps have been filled in, use the back of the rake to tamp down the joints to make sure they are in contact with the soil below.

Laying turf on a slope

In gardens where there is a steep gradient, turfing is the best way to create a lawn. Seed can be used, but in heavy rain the seed or young grass may be washed down the slope making it difficult for the lawn to establish.

Turf can also slip down the gradient after rainfall and should therefore be secured with wooden pegs. Lay the turf in the normal way but with the rows running up and down the slope rather than across, and push a peg through each turf into the soil. Do not push the pegs in completely, as otherwise they will be difficult to find and remove. As soon as the grass roots into the soil, the pegs can be pulled out.

1

2

3

4

5

Aftercare of Newly Laid Turf

Turf lawns are generally very easy to care for, and in good conditions the roots should grow into the soil very quickly. In dry weather this will mean keeping the turf and soil constantly moist.

Watering

This is the most important job to carry out once the turf has been laid, as it will shrink and dry out very quickly in warm, dry weather. Ideally, water the turf with a sprinkler immediately after laying until the turf and soil below are moist. You then need to keep an eye on the turf and, as soon as it looks like the surface is drying out, water again. During this time, try to avoid walking on the grass, as the watering will soften the soil and you may leave footprints on the lawn. To position the sprinkler tread very carefully or use a plank to walk on.

If you have laid the lawn in mid-summer, you will probably have to water daily for a couple of weeks until the roots of the new turves establish into the soil. The amount

Dealing with shrinkage

If the turf is allowed to dry out it will shrink and gaps will appear between the individual pieces. If this occurs, water the area thoroughly and when the turf is moist, gently stretch the pieces back into shape. If the turf cannot be stretched enough, mix together some top soil and compost and brush this into the gaps. Once the turf is established the gaps will eventually grow over.

A sprinkler is the most efficient method of giving a new lawn the water that it needs

and length of time you need to water will depend on the weather and soil conditions, but whatever the prevailing situation the turf must be kept moist at all times.

Mowing

Once the turf has knitted together it is time to give the lawn its first trim. However, do not be tempted to mow new turf until it is well and truly established. If you try to mow before the roots grow, the mower may tear up the turf. To tell if the turf has rooted successfully, give the grass a gentle tug; if you cannot lift it from the soil, then turf and soil have successfully knitted together. You will also notice that as the roots grow into the soil the lawn will become less spongy and will feel firmer due to the roots pulling the turf down to the ground.

For the first cut, you can use either a rotary or cylinder mower with the blades set high. Make sure you remove the grass clippings, either by catching them in the mower box or with a rake, so that they do not smother the new shoots of grass. Gradually lower the blade height over the next three or

If you do not mow with a box, be sure to rake up all grass cuttings

The 'tug test' is the best way of ensuring that new turves have rooted successfully

four cuts, as the lawn becomes ever more established and the grass becomes accustomed to being mowed regularly.

Rolling is not normally necessary, although the light roller often found on the back of a mower will help to keep the surface of the lawn firm.

Weeding and feeding

If you have used good quality turf in your lawn, weeds should not be a problem. However, you may find the occasional weed in some grades of turf, and these should be cut out by hand. If existing weeds in the soil were not killed before laying the lawn, they can grow through the turf; again, remove the offenders by hand.

Feeding should not be needed for several months if a fertilizer was applied for the first time during soil preparation. After six months the lawn should be established enough to use a feed and weed, and then it is a good idea to make this a regular task.

LAWN MAINTENANCE

A lawn is very often the one part of the garden that is taken for granted, receiving little more than a regular cut to keep it in trim. People feed their house plants, planted containers, hanging baskets, vegetables and roses, but in many cases the lawn is left to fend for itself, resulting in a poor quality lawn that is full of weeds. Lawns are made up of growing plants and just like any other plants in the garden they need water, light, nutrients and oxygen to grow properly.

When you consider that in just 1 sq m (1 sq yd) of lawn there can be between 10,000 and 15,000 grass plants all requiring water and nutrients, you will see that there is a definite need to maintain your lawn!

How much Maintenance?

Maintaining a fine lawn in top quality will require more work than that required on a family lawn, but with modern fertilizers, weedkillers and garden machinery,

Regularly spiking the lawn to aerate the soil will help the grass to grow more strongly

maintenance is much simpler nowadays and can be both very satisfying and not too demanding on time. The amount of maintenance that you give to a lawn will depend on several factors, including:

• the quality of the lawn you want to create
• the time you have available
• the size of the lawn
• the cost of maintenance

The very minimum of work that should be done is regular mowing and trimming of the edges and an occasional feed with a lawn fertilizer. Ideally, feeding should be done in spring and again in autumn to maintain healthy and strong growth. At the other extreme you could go for a full maintenance programme as would be carried out on a fine turf sports surface, such as a bowling green or golf green. This involves much more work, and as well as mowing and feeding you will be carrying out weed control, aeration, scarifying, top dressing, discouraging pests and many other procedures throughout the year. The result, however, will be a lawn of superlative quality.

Most people wanting to create or maintain a lawn to a good standard opt for a midway approach and will carry out the basic requirements to keep the lawn looking good, with a few other jobs thrown in as and when needed.

An electric edging tool-cum-strimmer makes light of this job

Mowing

The majority of time spent working on a lawn is devoted to mowing. It is done to maintain the grass at a set height and to make the lawn look attractive. Regular mowing also helps to thicken out the sward to give a dense covering. The amount of mowing needed will depend on the type of lawn, the finish that you want to create, the amount of rainfall or irrigation and soil and air temperature. In some areas this can mean mowing from early-spring until late-autumn, whereas in other areas where the climate is very mild mowing can almost be an all-year-round job.

Mowing should always be determined by the state of the grass growth and weather, rather than the calendar. The busiest mowing times are usually in late spring and early summer, when the ground is warm and moist. At this time grass growth is usually very fast. During mid- to late summer, when it can be very hot and the soil dry, grass growth will be much slower, especially if the lawn is not watered. During the winter, grass growth is very slow and in sub-zero temperatures grass stops growing completely for short periods. During the coldest of the winter months mowing is not normally required.

Regular mowing is the most basic and essential part of lawn maintenance

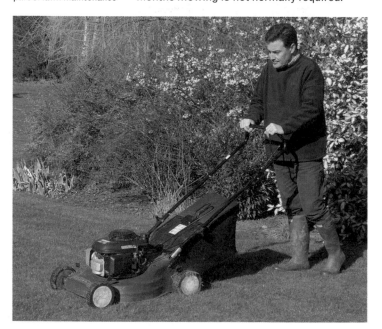

How much to Cut Off?

The grass mixture and desired finish will determine the height of cut on the lawn. Generally speaking, lawns made from fine-leaved grasses such as fescues and bents are mown closer than lawns with ryegrass.

Fine lawn

On a domestic lawn the lowest you are likely to mow a quality fine lawn to is around 5mm (¼in) although 12mm (½in) is more usual.

Buy a mower with a fully adjustable height of cut and alter it according to your lawn's requirements

Mowing too close can weaken the grass and encourage moss and weeds to establish.

Family lawn

For an all-purpose family lawn, the mowing height ranges from 12–50mm (½–2in) depending on the circumstances. The average height is around 25mm (1in) but mowing the grass slightly higher will help to protect against heavy wear such as children playing ball games.

How Often to Mow?

With all lawns it is always better to mow little and often rather than giving an occasional cut where large amounts of grass are lopped off in one go. Not only is

Swishing the dew

If the lawn is covered with heavy dew, it is best to wait until the lawn has dried to make mowing easier, or you can brush the lawn to disperse the dew. Green keepers who cannot wait for the grass to dry naturally 'swish' the grass with a long, flexible fibre-glass cane. Not only does this allow you to mow early in the morning, the removal of water from the blades of grass is a good way of discouraging some lawn diseases that thrive in moist conditions. In a garden situation a long bamboo cane can be used to swish along the surface of the lawn before mowing.

cutting long grass hard work, cutting it severely is much more stressful for the lawn and recovery time will take longer. For the person who does not care about his lawn this may not pose a problem, but if you want your lawn to look good, it is best to avoid allowing the lawn to grow long and then suddenly scalping it. A tell-tale sign that a lawn has been mown too close is the colour. Instead of a lush green it will take on a very pale, almost white appearance. Regular mowing in which approximately one third to a half of the grass is removed will keep the lawn looking green and recovery will be faster.

The Mowing Year

Spring Mowing normally commences in spring. For the first few cuts, leave the grass a little longer and as the season progresses gradually lower the height of the cut to the required height. In peak growing times – when you can almost see the grass growing before your eyes – mowing may be needed more than once a week; however, this is not always possible due to other commitments.

Summer As spring turns into summer the growth of the lawn will settle down and mowing will be needed less frequently. However, where time permits it is advisable to still mow once a week even if it only means removing a small amount of grass. When grass growth really slows down in hot dry weather, it may be several weeks between cuts, and in these conditions the height of cut should be raised slightly. Raising the blades will help to keep the grass greener for longer.

Autumn and winter In autumn the grass growth will gradually slow down as the soil and air temperatures drop, which means that mowing is required less frequently. During the winter months, if the grass is growing there is no reason why it should not be mown, providing the conditions are favourable – that is, not wet, snowy or frosty. To keep the lawn neat and tidy usually all that is needed is an occasional topping with the blades set fairly high.

TIP Mowing should never be done when the lawn is covered in frost as the grass will be damaged. Likewise you should not mow in very wet conditions as otherwise the ground will be compacted by the mower and by you walking on it, and the mower will clog with grass cuttings.

Never mow a frosty lawn – you will greatly damage the grass

Dealing with Grass Clippings

There are no hard and fast rules when it comes to collecting grass clippings from the lawn, but there are some advantages and disadvantages to both. Generally speaking you will get a much better quality lawn if the clippings are collected for the majority of the time. This will make the lawn look much neater and it also removes seed heads from weed grasses and broad-leaved weeds.

When clippings are left the lawn will not look as attractive, as the clippings start to die and grass is constantly carried indoors on feet. The lawn is also more likely to have a high worm population due to the decaying grass clippings in the base of the lawn. This can cause problems, as some worms produce casts of soil that are pushed up onto the surface of the lawn. Not only does this look unsightly, it can also make mowing more difficult. However, on heavy clay soils encouraging worms to tunnel through the soil will help with drainage and aeration.

A build up of clippings over a season will make the lawn spongy and thatch will develop in the base of the lawn. This in turn can trap moisture and lead to fungal diseases, especially during the autumn

There are times when it is best to leave the box off the mower and the clippings behind on the lawn

Grass clippings: pros and cons

Pros:
- returns nutrients to soil
- acts as mulch to retain moisture
- encourages worms, which help to aerate clay soils

Cons:
- looks untidy
- may cause fungal diseases
- encourages worms which can leave unsightly 'casts'
- helps to propagate weed seeds

months. However, during periods of drought grass clippings left on the lawn can act as a mulch and help to retain moisture in the soil – very important if irrigation is not available.

Grass clippings also contain valuable nutrients that are lost when they are collected. If left on the lawn the nutrients are returned to the soil. It is estimated that by leaving the grass clippings on your lawn the recycled nutrients equate to around one quarter of the amount needed by the lawn.

Mowing with a box is the quickest and easiest way to pick up cuttings

Choosing a Mower

To make caring for your lawn easier it is important to have the right mower to suit your lawn or circumstances, but before rushing out to buy a new mower have a good look at the many different mowers that are available. The numerous different options can seem a little daunting at first, but it helps to break down the choice into two main considerations:

• how is the mower best powered?
• what kind of cutting action do I want?

Electric, petrol or push?

The first thing to decide is whether you want an electric, petrol or push mower. Electric mowers come in many designs and are usually cheaper than their petrol alternatives. There is no messing about with petrol or checking oil and filters and electric mowers are generally much lighter. To use them you need to have an electric supply close by with a circuit breaker fitted for safety. Electric mowers are ideal for small to medium sized lawns, whereas with a petrol mower you can mow very large areas as you are not restricted by a cable. Petrol mowers are more expensive, but they will last for many years if looked after properly and modern petrol engines are much easier to start and maintain than older engines. Push mowers are suitable for small areas and require no petrol or electricity, just a little effort from you!

Cylinder or rotary?

Then there is the choice between a cylinder and rotary mower. A cylinder mower cuts with a scissor-like action as the cylinder blade by-passes the fixed bottom blade; the higher the number of blades on the cylinder, the finer the cut. The finish with a cylinder mower is very good and they are ideal for people who want a quality lawn. A rotary mower, on the other hand, has a horizontal blade or set of blades that rotate at a high speed to cut the grass.

Types of Mower

If possible, try to borrow a mower first to see what type of job it does on a lawn and whether it is suitable for your needs.

Hover mowers

This design of mower has no wheels or rollers; it simply glides on a cushion of air making it very easy to handle – but obviously you would not choose a hover mower if you wanted to create stripes across the lawn! Hover mowers are a type of rotary mower, because the action of the blade and the finish of cut is similar to those of a conventional rotar lawnmower.

The majority of models are powered by electricity and are suitable for small to medium lawns, but larger petrol models are also available that are ideal for mowing grass banks where it is difficult to take other types of mowers. The electric models are

Hover mowers are light, manoeuvrable and powered by electricity

Size matters

Remember: big is not always the best option. Mowers start from around 30cm (12in) wide and go up to 120cm (48in). For small lawns, choose a small mower and a larger mower for a large lawn. Many people make the mistake of buying a large mower for a small lawn, thinking that it will take less time to cut the grass. In many cases it can be the opposite, as a large mower is more difficult to manoeuvre in a tight space and around beds, borders and trees planted in the lawn.

A petrol rotary mower is versatile, durable and good for medium to large lawns

light to handle and can be stored by hanging them by their handle – very handy if you have limited storage space.

On the smaller models like the one pictured on the previous page, the blades are often made from plastic and can be changed in a matter of seconds without the need for tools. It is the speed at which they rotate that cuts the grass. Normally it is not possible to alter the height of the blade, although with some of the larger petrol models you can use spacers behind the blade to change the height of cut. Some hover mowers have been adapted to collect grass clippings, but the majority do not, and they work best when the lawn is cut little and often.

Petrol rotary mowers

This type of mower is very robust and will last for many years. They cut with a steel rotating blade and can be used to mow both short and long grass. Some models need to be pushed whereas others are self-propelled. There are various designs, with some having four wheels and others with two front wheels and a rear roller so that you can stripe your lawn. Height adjustment is made on the wheels or roller. Rotary mowers can be used with or without the grass box and are suitable for medium to large lawns and will give a good finish.

Electric rotary mowers

These are now one of the most popular types of mower and are ideal for small to medium-sized lawns. The size of the electric motor will determine the power and it pays to go for a high wattage machine. This will be more able to cope with heavy mowing

An electric rotary mower is suitable for smaller lawns only

conditions. They are much lighter than the petrol equivalent, which is a benefit if you find petrol mowers too heavy. Some models have four wheels and others have a real roller to stripe the grass. Most types have rear grass collection.

Cylinder mowers

For lawns that are normally mown fairly short and on a regular basis, a cylinder mower is perfect and will give a lovely striped lawn. If the grass is allowed to grow long, mowing with a cylinder mower can be difficult, as the front roller flattens the grass. In this situation you may need to mow more than once, gradually lowering the cut. To adjust the height of cut you can move the cylinder and bottom blades up and down; on modern mowers this is usually done with a handle or wheel on the side of the machine.

Most cylinder mowers also have a rear roller which stripes the lawn as you mow. To cut well the blade needs to be properly adjusted and you have to be very careful not to hit any obstructions that might damage

Push mowers are light, handy and easy to use.

TIP

To help you mow a straight line, pick an object at the opposite end of the lawn and keeping your eye on the object mow towards it, rather than looking at the grass in front of the mower. With a little practice you will soon be able to mow in a perfectly straight line.

the blade. The grass is thrown forward into the collection box on the front, which can be removed if you wish. Models are available from a 30cm (12in) cut up to 60cm (24in), making them suitable for lawns of all sizes. The petrol models tend to be heavier and produce a bolder stripe, but several companies also make electric cylinder mowers which are very effective.

Push mowers

This type of mower is not as popular nowadays, although they are still available from some companies. They are inexpensive to buy and will last for many years. Although they look a little basic, they do a good job with their small cutting cylinder. Push mowers are ideal for small lawns but the grass does need to be mown regularly as they are hard work to use on long grass. They are also a good way of getting some exercise in the garden!

A cylinder mower equipped with a roller is the best choice if you wish to create a striped effect

If you have a large lawn, a ride-on mower could be the one for you

Ride-on mowers

Both cylinder and rotary models are available, with the rotary types being the most popular by far. These mowers are excellent for cutting large areas of lawn and are available with or without collection boxes. The rear collectors are better if the grass is a little damp, as those that blow the grass up a plastic tube at the side soon tend to block. Many also have a roller on the collector which creates broad stripes across the lawn. Cutting widths start from around 90cm (36in) and go up to around 120cm (48in), and most models are now electric start for ease of use.

Mulching mowers

This is a type of rotary mower that instead of collecting the mown grass cuts it into fine mulch; this is then blown down into the base of the lawn. The idea is to reduce mowing time and the amount of grass clippings that are dumped into landfill sites. These mowers work by having a modified blade that cuts the grass and then continues to chop it into very small pieces. Mulching mowers are perfectly effective as long as you mow on a dry day and the grass is not too long. However, if the grass is wet and long, the mulching effect does not work properly and the grass will remain on the surface of the lawn; in order to work effectively, mowing needs to be done on a regular basis. The downside of a mulch mower is that after a couple of seasons the

Mower matters

• With all types of mower, always wear strong foot wear.

• Always make sure the mower is running correctly and that the blades are properly adjusted. Cylinder blades that do not meet with the bottom blade will chew the grass; blunt rotary blades will cut the grass in such a way as to cause a rough edge that will dry to leave brown tips.

• Check the lawn for any stones or objects that may damage the mower or people close by.

• If the mower is a petrol model, check the oil and fuel. If more petrol needs adding to the tank, do not do this on the lawn, as spilled petrol will kill the grass.

• When mowing with an electric mower it is always advisable to use an RCD plug as an extra safety measure; in the event of accidentally cutting through the cable, the power is automatically turned off.

grass can become very soft and spongy. It is also thought that using this type of mower might result in a build up of thatch in the lawn, but as the grass is chopped very finely and decomposes quickly, this really should not be a problem. One advantage of this kind of mower is that less fertilizer is needed on a lawn mown with a mulch mower, as the nutrients in the clippings are continually being recycled.

How to Mow

Most mowers are designed to be pushed forwards along the lawn, although when mowing a grassy bank with a hover mower it is often easier to use an action that involves swinging the mower from side to side.

Rectangular or square lawns

First mow a strip at both ends of the lawn, usually two widths of the mower, to create a turning area. Then mow up and down the length of the garden in straight lines or following the curve of a border. When mowing the second strip, overlap the previous strip slightly in order to prevent leaving any un-mown grass between the two strips. After using the mower for a short while, you will soon get the feel of the machine and be able to judge the mowing width and overlap required to do the job effectively without missing any bits. If the mower has a roller, the lawn will be striped as you mow up and down.

Circular or irregular shaped lawns

For circular lawns or those of an unusual shape, the mowing technique is very similar in that you should first mow a couple of strips around the edge of the lawn. Then mow a straight line down the centre of the lawn – or at the longest point from end to end – to form a mowing guide before mowing each half.

It also benefits the lawn if you can mow in a different direction each time you mow. This prevents wheel or roller marks that can develop if you always mow exactly the same way, and it encourages a thicker sward as the grass is not continuously being rolled in one direction in the process of mowing.

Mow even strips allowing for overlap and turning space

Feeding

A lawn will grow for many years without being supplied with additional fertilizer, surviving on the nutrient reserve in the soil, but for the best results the grass should be fed once or twice a year to keep the lawn looking green and healthy. Lawns that are hungry will be a pale green colour instead of a deep green, have a thinner grass cover and usually have a higher population of weeds and mosses. The lawn will also be less hard-wearing and more prone to certain turf diseases that thrive in poor growing conditions. Although feeding will encourage stronger growth in spring and early summer, the advantages to be gained far out-weigh the effort of having to mow the lawn a couple of extra times over a season.

The application of lawn fertilizer has never been easier and many manufacturers supply the feed in handy spreaders to make application simple. Many are also combined with a moss killer and weedkiller to enable you to carry out three operations in one go.

Nutrients

There are several mixes of nutrients available for feeding at different times of the year and it is important that the correct nutrients are used at the right time.

For healthy growth, the three main nutrients needed by grass are nitrogen (N), phosphorous (P) and potassium (K) and although these are naturally present in the soil, due to the high rate that they are used when the grass is growing they are the ones that need topping up.

Nitrogen is essential for leaf growth and plays a major role in the production of Chlorophyll, which makes the leaves green. When there is a shortage of nitrogen the leaves will become pale and yellow and growth will be weak and stunted. During spring and summer when the lawn is growing at its fastest, nitrogen is needed in large amounts to maintain healthy growth and fast recovery after mowing or heavy wear. Nitrogen is easily washed through the soil by winter rains or irrigation and therefore needs to be re-applied on a regular basis in order to keep the levels in the soil topped up.

> **TIP**
> The use of high nitrogen fertilizer should stop at the end of the summer, since you do not want to encourage soft, lush grass growth during the autumn as this is more prone to fungal diseases.

Phosphorus is required in smaller amounts and is mainly needed to establish root growth. The better the root system, the better the top growth will be. A healthy root system also means the plants are better prepared to withstand cold and wet winter conditions and dry conditions in the summer. A phosphorus deficiency in grass is rare and is recognized by a purple edge to the leaf.

Potassium is important and although not needed in large amounts it plays an important role in the plant's metabolism. It

Lawn Nutrients

Nutrient	Needed for	When most needed	Shortage leads to
Nitrogen	leaf growth	spring/summer	pale, yellow leaves
Phosphorous	root growth	autumn	purple edge to leaves
Potassium	plant metabolism	all year	brown tips to leaves

helps to regulate growth and induces winter hardiness, drought and disease resistance. Again, a deficiency is very unusual in a lawn situation, but occasionally shows as brown tips to the leaves, which should not be confused with brown cut tips after mowing.

Other elements such as calcium, sulphur, magnesium are also essential for plant growth and the manufacturing of cells and proteins within the plant, but these are normally only required in small amounts and are present in most soils.

Trace elements or micro-elements such as iron, copper, boron, manganese, zinc and molybdenum are needed in very small amounts and these do not need to be added under normal growing conditions as they are also naturally available in the soil. Iron is however often added to a lawn feed as it acts as a tonic and makes the grass green without promoting lush growth.

Types of Lawn Fertilizer

There are two main types of fertilizer that can be applied to your lawn and these contain a mixture of the nutrients best suited to the season and growth requirements. Different manufacturers may give them different names, but basically the two categories are spring/summer feeds and autumn feeds.

For ease of application, most lawn fertilizers are mini-granules that are sprinkled evenly over the surface of the lawn. Concentrated liquid fertilizer that is diluted and watered onto the lawn is also available, as is soluble powdered fertilizer that is dissolved with water and applied to the lawn.

Spring/summer feed
Fertilizers designated 'spring/ summer feed' have a high nitrogen content. Start to apply these feeds when the lawn begins to make new growth in the spring, and continue while the grass is actively growing through to the end of summer.

The nitrogen is essential for leaf growth and will quickly turn a pale lawn a healthy green colour. During the growing season nitrogen is needed the most, as every time the lawn is cut, nitrogen is used to make new growth. Although some of the spring and summer fertilizers contain only nitrogen, most also have a percentage of the other main nutrients and a typical analysis might be 12:5:5 (N:P:K). The ratio will vary from manufacturer to manufacturer, but nitrogen will always be the highest percentage.

For convenience, many spring/summer granular feeds also have a weed killer and or moss killer added. This means that with just one application you can feed the lawn, control broad-leaved weeds and moss.

Autumn feed
The autumn lawn fertilizers are designed to strengthen and build up the lawn in preparation for the cold winter months. Although the physical signs of autumn feeding are not as evident as a spring feed that encourages strong green growth, the lawn will certainly benefit from the feed. The lawn will be able to withstand the harsh winter weather and will be in a healthier condition to start into growth come spring.

Fast or slow release?

Many brands contain both fast and slow acting nitrogen that quickly green-up the grass and then continue to feed for several weeks or months. The high nitrogen liquid and soluble powdered feeds tend to be fast acting and are ideal for where you want a green lawn very quickly, but the nutrients are soon used and only last for around one to two weeks at the most. If you only want to make one spring/summer application choose a slow release lawn fertilizer that will last for three months and apply it in mid-spring.

Autumn lawn fertilizer contains a mixture of nutrients, but unlike the summer feeds, nitrogen is only supplied in a small amount. A typical N:P:K analysis of an autumn feed would be 4:10:5. This will encourage a good root system and induce winter hardiness, while still maintaining a healthy green colour. Very often the nutrients used in this type of feed are control released. In very cold weather when the grass stops growing the nutrients are held within the granule and only made available as the soil temperature starts to rise again.

Many autumn lawn feeds also contain a moss killer in the form of ferrous sulphate, which as well as controlling moss, also acts as a lawn tonic.

Applying Lawn Fertilizer

There are three mains ways to feed your lawn:

• by hand
• with a spreader
• by liquid feeding

Which method you use will depend on the size of the lawn and what kind of equipment you have available.

Whatever method you use, always read the instructions on the fertilizer packet first, thoroughly taking note of any special instructions, in particular watering in requirements and spreading rates. All the relevant information and application rates will be shown on the packet, plus a full break down of the nutrient ratio and any moss killers and weedkillers that are included.

Watering in If there is no rainfall within a given time, you may need to water in the fertilizer. Failure to do this may result in some scorching to the grass. Some types of fertilizer, especially the slow release ones, are less likely to scorch and do not always require watering in.

Spreading rates It is also important that the fertilizer is spread evenly and at the correct rate. This is less important with liquid feeding as the fertilizer has been diluted, but if granular feeds are applied at too high a rate the grass can be damaged.

Hand spreading

For small lawns the fertilizer can be spread by hand. Before applying the feed, work out the area of the lawn and calculate the amount of fertilizer needed. First spread half the quantity of fertilizer walking across the entire lawn in one direction, then spread the other half by walking across the lawn at 90-degrees. This will give a more even distribution across the lawn. If spreading the fertilizer by hand always wear gloves, scattering the fertilizer as you go. With a little practice you will soon be able to spread the fertilizer in an even pattern.

Another very easy and convenient method is to use one of the products that are supplied in a hand-held applicator. The

Spreading fertilizer by hand is quick and accurate, but it is advisable to wear gloves when handling this material

fertilizer is simply poured out of the container at the correct rate and is spread evenly across the grass as you walk forward. As the granules are normally light coloured, you can see where they fall on the lawn, which helps prevent overdosing.

Liquid fertilizer

There are several methods of applying liquid fertilizer to a lawn, and all are very easy. The simplest method is to buy lawn fertilizer in concentrated form in a hose-end feeder that simply clips onto the hose pipe. As water passes through, the fertilizer is diluted at the correct rate and watered over the lawn. This type of fertilizer is very fast acting and as well as feeding you are also watering, which means no scorch.

Another, similar method is to have a hose-end feeder that can be used for all types of feeding around the garden to which you add a soluble lawn fertilizer. Again, this dilutes the fertilizer as water passes through.

Fertilizer spreaders

For large lawns a mechanical spreader can be used to spread granular fertilizer. Two types are readily available.

Spinning spreaders have a hopper that is filled with the fertilizers and as you walk it

Applying liquid lawn feed by watering can is an effective but slow and time consuming method

drops through a hole onto a spinning plate that throws the fertilizer across the lawn in a circular pattern. These are ideal for large lawns.

Drop spreaders are very simple to use and are simply pushed up and down the lawn as if mowing. Fertilizer trickles though the base of the spread onto the lawn below and this can be regulated to change the application rate.

Fertilizer spreaders ensure an even, properly calibrated rate of distribution

Weed Control

No matter how well you care for your lawn, weeds can suddenly appear and start to grow. As a general rule, the thicker the grass sward and healthier the lawn, the more difficult it is for weeds to establish, but even then they still manage to find a way in.

Some people do not mind a few weeds in their lawn, whereas others wish the lawn to be totally weed free. To a certain extent it depends on the type of lawn you want to create. A closely mown, manicured lawn does look better without weeds, whereas a cared for family lawn will not be spoilt by the odd weed or two. In fact, lawn weeds or wildflowers can be used to create a feature within an existing lawn (see Wildflowers in the Lawn, pages 95–9).

Methods of Weed Control

There are several ways to kill weeds growing in your lawn and most weeds can be controlled by one or more methods, although some of them may require more than one treatment.

Even once you have made your lawn weed-free, there is no guarantee that weeds will not return, as they are spread by wind-borne seed, by bird droppings that contain seeds and creeping stems from nearby.

Hand weeding

Although this means physically getting down on your hands and knees to remove the weeds, it is an effective way of controlling just a few weeds on a small garden. In an established lawn, a small garden fork or blade can be used to ease out the roots of the weed. In the case of deep-rooted weeds, such as dandelion (*Taraxacum officinale*), severing the root will not kill the plant, as new growth will eventually grow from the remains of the root deep down.

Painting weeds individually with weedkiller is highly effective, but will take ages in all but the smallest garden

Weed and feed

This is perhaps one of the most popular methods of treating a lawn for weeds. The fertilizer also contains a selective herbicide that kills broad-leaved weeds but not the grass. The tiny granules rely on landing on the leaves of the weeds where it dissolves

Which weeds?

Certain weeds will not grow in lawns, especially taller growing perennials such as couch grass (*Agropyron repens*), docks (*Rumex obtusifolia*) and stinging nettles (*Urtica dioica*), as regular mowing will eventually kill them off. Many annuals such as chickweed (*Stellaria media*), groundsel (*Senecio vulgaris*) and fat hen (*Chenopodium album*) will also not grow in a lawn, and although these often appear in newly seeded lawns, after several cuts they will die off.

The weeds that do survive and thrive in lawns have adapted to regular mowing and either produce low growing rosettes, very small leaves that grow close to the soil, or have creeping stems that spread rapidly across the lawn (see Weeds Directory, pages 113–27).

and is absorbed into the weed. Although this method of control is fairly effective and easy to use, it does not work on all weeds, especially the ones that have very small leaves such as suckling clover (*Trifolium dubium*). One of the main advantages of using a feed and weed is that once the weeds have died the grass that has just been fed will quickly grow and fill the spaces left by the weeds.

Lawn sand

Lawn sand is not as widely used nowadays as a weedkiller although some green keepers still use it early in the season. Washed sand is used as the main carrier and to this Ferrous Sulphate and Ammonium Sulphate are added. The former scorches off the leaves of weeds, although it does not kill the roots and is an effective moss killer. The latter, which is high in nitrogen, greens the lawn up and makes it a lush green colour. Lawn sand is normally applied from early spring to early summer.

Liquid weedkiller

Concentrated liquid weedkiller is a very effective way of killing all broad-leaved lawn weeds, especially the small leaved types. The concentrate has to be diluted with water and can be applied through a watering can or by a sprayer. Where possible, always try to use a sprayer, as this gives a more even coverage across the lawn and the fine mist from the sprayer gives a better coating on the leaves of the weeds. The selective weedkiller in the spray will kill broad leaf weeds and their roots, but not grass. As well as the concentrated formula, ready to use handy sprayers are also available. These contain the diluted weedkiller mixture and are very convenient where you only have a small lawn or just a few weeds to spot treat.

Touch weeders

Several companies also make a touch weeder or weed pencil. This is a small plastic tube with a foam end that is used to dab the weed killer onto the weed. Again, this type of weed control is ideal for just one or two weeds.

Weedkillers: best practice

For best results when using lawn weedkillers, bear in mind the following points:

• Always use as directed on the label and never be tempted to increase the dose, as this may result in damage to the lawn.

• When using a selective lawn weedkiller, be careful not to get it on any ornamental plants as they will also be damaged.

• The best time to use any lawn weedkiller is when the weeds are actively growing. If using a liquid lawn weedkiller, it is a good idea to feed the lawn one week earlier to make sure the weeds are growing vigorously.

• When using a selective lawn weedkiller it is normal practice to mow the lawn three days before application and not again for at least three days afterwards to prevent possible scorching of the grass.

Handy liquid sprayers are good for killing occasional weeds

Dealing with Moss

There are several types of moss that grow in lawns, but they can all be treated in the same manner if you are trying to get rid of them. Although individual moss plants can look very attractive, in a lawn situation they can spoil the appearance and make mowing more difficult. They also make the lawn surface spongy, hold on to water which can encourage diseases and in severe infestations will smother the grass.

The two main types of moss that you find in lawns are Pleurocarpous and Acrocarpous. The pleurocarps are feathery in appearance and prefer longer grass and can often be controlled by mowing a little closer. The acrocarps are closer growing and often form a dense matt of moss. These are able to grow in very poor soils where conditions are damp or dry.

Mosses tend to be more of a problem during the cooler parts of the year and many species die off during the summer months. They reproduce by spores that are released during the spring and autumn and also by small pieces of the plant that become detached from the parent plant.

Moss growing in lawn grass is very unsightly and should be removed

Moss control

Moss growth on lawns is usually due to one or more of the following conditions:

• soil compaction
• poor surface drainage
• soils with very low fertility
• heavy shade
• acidic soils

Although getting rid of moss from a lawn is reasonably easy, unless you improve the growing conditions that cause the moss problem in the first place, the moss will simply return each year (see especially pages 19–24).

Once the moss is removed, the lawn will look somewhat worse for wear, but it will recover in time

Cultural control Various cultural methods can be used to give some degree of control, such as raising the height of cut slightly where the moss is encouraged by very close mowing, or by lowering the height of cut where tall feathery-type mosses are growing.

Total control For total control the moss needs to be killed and removed. The best time to do this is in late winter/early spring or autumn when the moss is growing.

Lawn Sand containing Sulphate of Ammonia and Ferrous Sulphate is a traditional method and works very well. The iron in the Ferrous Sulphate scorches off the moss and also acts as a tonic to the lawn, while the ammonia will give the grasses a boost in growth.

Scarifying

Lawns are scarified for several reasons. The main reason is to remove dead moss a couple of weeks after a moss killer has been applied and also to reduce 'thatch' in the lawn. Thatch is more of a problem in lawns that contain strong-growing grasses which spread by rhizomes and stolons, less so in lawns where the majority of the grasses have a tufted habit. Sacrifying helps to aerate the soil and improve surface drainage, leading to healthier and thicker grass.

TIP Scarifying little and often throughout the growing season will prevent thatch from building up in the base of a lawn, but avoid doing so during long periods of drought.

When to scarify

Scarifying is mainly done in the autumn and should be carried out when the soil is moist and still warm. This allows the grass time to recover and thicken out before the onset of winter. It can also be done in spring once the lawn has started to grow.

Many professional greenkeepers carry out a very light scarification during the summer months as a means of preventing thatch from building up and this can also be done in a garden situation, as long as the grass is growing and not suffering from drought.

How to scarify

There are two ways you can scarify your lawn: by hand or by machine. A wire lawn rake is a very effective method of removing dead moss and thatch on small lawns. The harder you press, the deeper the rake will go into the lawn, and in just a short time you will have a pile of debris. However, a mechanical scarifyer is much easier to use and these are available in many sizes and specifications to suit all lawns.

When using a mechanical scarifyer, start off shallow and then adjust the tines to go deeper

What is thatch?

Thatch is a layer of dead and decaying organic material that builds up in the base of the lawn on the surface of the soil. It consists of leaves, stems, dead moss, rhizomes, stolons and other plant material. Over a period of time the thatch layer can become very thick and create a soft spongy lawn.

Pros – small layer of thatch can be beneficial as it:
• protects the surface of the soil
• makes the lawn slightly harder wearing
• reduces water evaporation

Cons – a thick layer of thatch will:
• lead to poor surface drainage
• prevent irrigation penetrating the soil
• encourage weeds
• hamper air circulation and so encourage diseases

Scarifying by hand using a rake will get the job done, but the work is arduous and time consuming

Spiking

Spiking a lawn is done to allow air into the soil (aeration) which is essential for healthy root growth. It also helps to improve surface drainage and to relieve soil compaction as a result of heavy wear. It is not always necessary to spike the whole lawn, but certainly areas where growth is poor or where the soil remains wet should be given some attention.

Spiking is an easier and quicker job if you hire or buy a mechanical spiking machine

Hollow tine spiking

This method of spiking removes a core of soil approximately 1cm (½in) wide and up to 10cm (4in) deep. Hollow tining is quite a slow job, but the benefits are well worth the effort. Fortunately, spiking does not need to be done every year, and in a lawn situation is only done where there is a problem with grass growth or if you want to improve the top soil. Hand spikers can be used on small areas, but for very large lawns you may wish to hire a machine for the job. A mechanical spiker has tines on a wheel or roller and is powered by electricity or a petrol engine.

On very heavy clay soils where drainage is poor, hollow tining will help to improve drainage and on very free draining sandy soils it can also be carried out to improve the moisture holding capacity, when combined with brushing in top

Hollow tine spiking with a push spiker can be a long, slow process

dressing material (see Top Dressing, opposite).

Spike over the area, leaving a distance of approximately 10cm (4in) between rows, and sweep the resulting soil cores off the lawn. In most cases you should then fill the holes with a bulky top dressing, or where the soil is very clayey or compacted simply leave the holes empty to settle and fill in from the surrounding soil over the winter.

When to spike Hollow tining is mainly done in autumn when the ground is moist, which makes it much easier to push in the tine, but it can also be done in early spring to improve drainage on areas of the lawn where water stands after rain.

Solid tine spiking

Spiking the lawn with a solid tine such as a garden fork allows air into the soil, helps water to drain through the grass and will also relieve soil with compaction. When using a garden fork the tines should be pushed straight into the soil at least 10cm (4in) deep before tilting the fork backwards to let more air in and to raise the turf slightly.

Raising the turf slightly with the fork loosens soil and reduces compaction

> **TIP**
>
> Lawns around newly built houses benefit greatly from spiking, as very often you will find that the soil has been compacted during the building process.

Top Dressing

A lawn top dressing is a bulky material that is applied to the surface of the lawn to produce a level surface and to add fresh soil to the holes created by hollow tining. Working this material into the base of the lawn also encourages new roots to develop and discourages a build up of thatch. Top dressing need not be done on an annual basis, but certainly where you are trying to improve an existing lawn or where the underlying soil is poor, it is worth carrying out this job fairly regularly.

How to top dress

For most lawns a proprietary top dressing available in bags is perfectly fine. This is usually a free-draining mixture of sieved soil and coarse sand. If your soil is heavy clay and standing water is a problem in some areas sharp sand on its own can be used to improve surface drainage. On very open, sandy soils where you want to try and retain moisture during the summer months, a loamy soil can be used. Some mixtures contain peat or a peat-free alternative, but avoid too much organic matter in the top-dressing as this will naturally decompose in the soil. If there is a

TIP

Never smother the grass with top dressing, as this will kill the grass and encourage fungal diseases. Make sure you wait until the grass is totally dry: if you try to spread the dressing in wet conditions you will make a sticky mess!

Use a shovel to scatter the top dressing as evenly as possible across the lawn

high level of organic matter, as it breaks down the soil is more likely to settle and the lawn will become uneven. Organic matter also holds on to water around the base of the plant which may lead to disease problems.

Choose a dry day and wait for the dew to dry on the grass. Spread the top dressing with a spade or shovel trying to scatter it as evenly as possible across the surface of the lawn. Use a stiff brush or broom and work the top dressing into the holes if you hollow tined and down into the base of the grass.

Seasonal dressings

Autumn dressing Apply top dressing as part of the autumn maintenance after scarifying and spiking, using the following quantities as a guideline:

• after solid tining – 1 kg/sq m (2lb/sq yd)
• after hollow tining – at least 3kg/sq m (6lb/sq yd), depending on the depth of the tines

Spring dressing A light top dressing can also be applied in mid-spring, but only if the lawn was not top dressed in the autumn

Use a stiff brush to work the dressing into the holes made during spiking, until all the dressing has disappeared

Over-seeding

Over-seeding is a technique that is used by professional greenkeepers to maintain the correct seed mixture in an area of turf.

Why over-seed?

Over time, some grass species die out and, unless these are replaced, the lawn will loose some of its qualities. You cannot tell precisely which grasses have died out, but if the lawn seems to change characteristics and some types of grass become more prominent, the chances are that some species have died out; over-seeding helps to keep a good balance of grasses. By maintaining a thick healthy sward the lawn will not only look better, it will also reduce weed invasion.

Over-seeding can also be done to improve an existing lawn by introducing new grass types that are more suitable for the type of lawn you require. For example, if currently you have a decorative fine lawn but would like it to become more hardwearing and multi-purpose, you can over-seed it with a tougher seed mix. You cannot, however, transform a hardwearing lawn into a fine lawn using this method.

How to over-seed

Over-seed in spring or autumn immediately after applying a top dressing. Sprinkle grass seed of the mixture that you require over the whole area at approximately 25g (¾ oz) per

Scratch the seed gently into the topsoil with a rake so that it has a chance to 'take'

During dry weather conditions, water the seed in thoroughly using a watering can or sprinkler

Sprinkle the new seed by hand to ensure that it goes where you want it

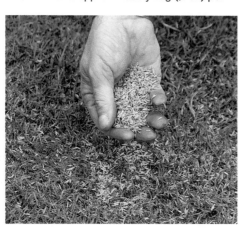

sq m (sq yd). Then lightly rake the seed into the surface of the lawn with a wire rake so that it is in contact with the top-dressing. If the weather is dry, irrigate the lawn with a watering can fitted with a rose or a sprinkler to aid germination.

Although all of the grass seed will not germinate, enough should and if this process is repeated over two seasons, you will notice changes in the appearance of your lawn.

Even if your lawn seems in good order, it is still worth over-seeding every two or three years. This way you will maintain a good supply of new healthy grass within the lawn, as it is estimated that in an average lawn up to 20 per cent of the individual grass plants die out each year.

Edging

Keeping the edges of a lawn neat and tidy is an essential maintenance task and when done it makes the lawn and surrounding garden look much better. The more you edge the easier and faster the job becomes: you should aim to trim the edges every time you mow or at least every other time.

The two main tools needed to keep your edges looking good are a half-moon edging iron and a pair of long handled shears. Some strimmers can also be used to maintain the edges (see page 73).

Vertical cutting

A half moon edging iron is designed to cut a new edge and is not normally used on a regular basis. The shape of the blade that gives the tool its name is pushed vertically into the ground at the edge of the lawn.

For a straight line, you can use a tight string line or a wooden board as a guide to cut the edge. Around a curved border you may be able to cut the shape by eye, although a rope or hose-pipe laid down to form the shape makes cutting much easier.

Trimming the edges with a half-moon is normally done during the winter or early spring in preparation for the coming season.

Use a plank as a straight-edge guide to ensure a neat line of cut

TIP
If you trim the edges before you mow with a rotary mower and then run the mower close to the lawn edge, the suction of the mower will collect most of the fine clippings.

Maintaining the edge

Use long-armed shears to trim the grass growth along the edge of the lawn. Providing you have cut a vertical edge with the half-moon, this job is very quick and easy. To save having to collect the grass clippings it is possible to fit a rubber trough on the lower blade for the clippings to fall into. In order for these gadgets to work efficiently, you need to trim the lawn edges regularly.

Tidy up straggly edges with long-handled shears or a strimmer

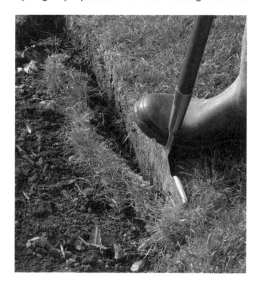

Edging the lawn with a half-moon cutter makes one of the most instant transformations possible in the garden

Brushing

Lawns do not need to be brushed regularly, but if you do have time to sweep the lawn occasionally it does benefit the grass at any time of the year. Greenkeepers brush regularly to disperse morning dew. This not only makes mowing easier, it helps to prevent some fungal diseases that prefer moist conditions. Brushing on a dry day also helps to get rid of worm casts that can be a problem on some lawns. They use a wide brush or a long, fine fibreglass cane that is swished along the surface of the lawn, hence the term 'swishing'. A similar effect can be achieved with a long garden cane on the home lawn.

Collecting Leaves

In the autumn as the leaves fall from the trees it is important to brush and collect them from the surface of the lawn. If left for long periods they block the light and turn the grass yellow, which in turn encourages diseases to set in. Leaves left on the lawn also encourage worms that pull the leaves down into the soil. Leaves can be brushed off by hand, blown into a corner or collected with a garden vacuum, before being added to a compost bin to rot down.

It is important to rake fallen leaves off the lawn before they damage the grass by blocking out light

Leaf-blowers are useful devices for getting leaves rounded up

Irrigation

Grass, like all living things, needs water in order to survive, and in periods of dry weather during the summer months lawns can suffer greatly. Fortunately, most grasses that are used in lawn mixtures nowadays are very resilient, and even though they may turn brown in hot, dry weather, they usually green-up again when the weather turns cooler and damp. Because of the good recovery time of most modern lawn grasses, many people choose not to water their lawns at all in order to save water. There is nothing wrong with this approach, as long as you do not mind the lawn looking somewhat straw-coloured at certain times of the year. The drawback of not watering in drought conditions is that the lawn is more likely to be invaded by strong growing weed-grasses and drought tolerant broad-leaved weeds, resulting in a poor quality lawn. Not only will the quality of the lawn suffer, but you will be faced with a whole host of new problems to address.

At the opposite extreme, some people water their lawn far too much and most of the water drains away and is wasted. However, by applying the correct amount of water at the right time, you can keep your lawn green and healthy in dry weather.

Spotting signs of drought

Grass leaves consist of approximately 85% water, so that when the soil dries out and the plant roots are unable to take in moisture, the leaves will lose their glossy green colour and take on a dark matt appearance. This is quickly followed by browning of the leaves. The time to irrigate is at the first sign of water shortage, when you spot the grass turning the tell-tale dark matt green. If swift action is taken, then the grass will recover very quickly and remain green.

A lawn suffering from drought is a sad sight indeed. Keep lawns well irrigated

When to Water

When and how often you need to water your lawn will vary from area to area, depending upon soil type, local climate and the grass types that you have chosen to grow in your garden. The best time of the day to water is generally in the early morning or the late evening when the ground is cooler, in order

A sprinkler is a good investment for anyone who owns a lawn

Monitor rainfall using a rain gauge in order to assess how much water your lawn needs

to reduce the amount of water lost through evaporation.

Sandy soils drain freely and their small reserve of water is quickly used up by the plants. Heavy clay soils, on the other hand, retain water in the soil and dry out much more slowly. The species of grasses growing in the lawn also affects when water is needed, as some are less tolerant of dry conditions than others. The level of mowing applied also plays its part and as a rule the closer you mow the faster the soil will dry out, because more water is lost through surface evaporation.

How Much Water?

There is no set rule for how much water your lawn needs, but the aim is to keep the top 10–15cm (4–6in) moist, as this is where the majority of the plants' roots are situated.

When watering your lawn, it is much better to give the grass a good soaking once every seven to ten days than it is to water little and often. If a small amount of water is applied every few days, the moisture will not penetrate down far into the soil. Instead, only the top 3–4cm (1½in) will be properly moist, which encourages shallow rooting of the grass. In some cases, the roots of the grass will actually grow up in search of water and if the soil then dries out the plants will show the effects of drought much faster. By giving the ground a good soaking on a regular basis, the water will be able to soak down further and the roots will grow downwards into the soil in search of it.

As a guide, 12mm (½in) of rain will soak into the soil approximately 10cm (4in), depending on the condition and type of soil, and this is the amount of water you should aim to supply when watering the lawn. You can very easily check this amount by positioning a rain gauge on the lawn, or by simply using a few empty jam-jars spread across the lawn, in order to measure the amount of water applied.

How to Water

The easiest and fastest way to water a lawn is with a hose pipe and sprinkler. The type of sprinkler you use will depend on the size and shape of your lawn.

Watering with a hand sprinkler is an effective method, as long as your lawn is not too large

Sprinklers come in a variety of different designs and configurations and take the pain out of lawn watering

Oscillating sprinklers are ideal for square or rectangular shaped lawns. They can usually be adjusted to alter the area covered by the spray and they provide a gentle watering pattern.

Static sprinklers are simple but effective. They are pushed into the ground and have a circular watering pattern. Normally they cannot be adjusted, but by turning the tap up or down you will alter the pressure of the water and thus the diameter of the spray.

Pulse-jet sprinklers also water in a circular pattern, but they can be adjusted in several ways. The watering diameter can be altered and they can also be adjusted to water a quarter, half or three-quarters of a circle on the lawn.

Watering by hand

For small areas where you do not want to use a sprinkler, the lawn can be watered by hand with a hose pipe. This gives you greater control of the watering, as you are able to apply more water to the driest

patches of the lawn with accuracy and total control. The disadvantage of watering in this way is that you always think you have applied more water than you actually have. Consequently, once again it is a good idea to use some type of rain gauge in order to measure the amount of water that has actually been dispensed.

Automatic watering

Fitting a small water timer to your tap will make watering the lawn a good deal easier. These are inexpensive to buy and run on batteries. They can be programmed to run for a set amount of time and will then switch off automatically, making them ideal for when you want to start watering late in the evening and go to bed with the knowledge that your lawn will be watered properly. They are also particularly useful devices for keeping grass and other plants alive when you go away for a few days.

Porous pipes These are made from a type of recycled rubber that allows water to seep through the sides of the pipe into the root area of the lawn, maintaining a moist soil. The main advantage of this type of irrigation is that it uses less water overall, as there is no surface evaporation.

A timer attached to the outside tap will ensure regular irrigation

Pop up sprinklers are especially useful for large lawns

Re-wetting dry soils

If your lawn has become very dry, it can be difficult to get water to soak down into the soil. One way to help water penetrate the soil is to lightly prick the area with a fork or use a shallow lawn spiker.

   Porous pipes can be installed into an existing lawn, but it is easier and less disruptive to install them before laying the turf. The pipes should be buried approximately 15cm (6in) deep so that spiking will not damage them and between 30–35cm (12–18in) apart.

Pop-up sprinklers As used on golf courses, these can also be installed on large lawns. They sit below the level of the lawn, and when the water is turned on the pressure pushes them up above the lawn where they then water in a set pattern. This type of irrigation is plumbed in permanently and is quite expensive to install. You also need very good water pressure in order to run the sprinkler effectively.

   Greenkeepers also use a 'wetting agent', which is a type of mild detergent that reduces the surface tension of water, thus helping it to soak into dry soils. Although wetting agents are not readily available

from garden centres, it is worth trying to find some if you have a particularly severe problem with dry soil. Alternatively, a few drops of washing up liquid in a watering can watered over the area will help.

   Another possible cause of water not soaking in is a disorder known as 'dry patch', which is quite common on areas of fine turf growing on sandy soil. The symptoms are dry areas of grass surrounded by green healthy grass (see Lawn Diseases, page 138).

   If 'dry patch' is a problem on your lawn, this is one area where washing-up water or bath water can be used because it contains a mild detergent. The contents of an average bath is enough to water a large area of the lawn and it can easily be syphoned from the bath by using a hose pipe.

TIP

Before using a hose pipe and sprinkler to water your lawn, particularly in periods of dry weather, it is well worth checking first with your local water authority to make sure there is not a hose pipe ban in place. In certain areas, a licence is also needed for watering with a sprinkler.

Complete Lawn Tools

It is possible to maintain a lawn with nothing more than a lawn mower, but most people usually have a few other pieces of equipment that help to keep the lawn in good condition. The range of tools and equipment available for use on lawns at various times of the year is wide, and as people become more interested in maintaining a good quality, healthy lawn, the more pieces they add to their collection. By no means do you need them all, and in many cases you can borrow items such as a fertilizer spreader from a garden centre if you purchase the fertilizer from them, or you can hire a scarifyer or spiker for a few days.

The amount of equipment that you end up accumulating will depend on the size of the lawn and the amount of work that you intend to do to it, in order to achieve a particular quality of finish.

Lawn Care Equipment: the Top 6

The following items are the basic equipment needed to keep a lawn in good condition, enabling you to carry out a wide range of maintenance tasks throughout the year, such as keeping the lawn trim, scarifying, aeration, weed control and edging.

Mower This is without doubt the most important piece of equipment needed to maintain your lawn. Ideally, lawns should be mown on a regular basis. Cutting little and often is not only better for the lawn, it also make it much easier for you to cut the grass. The choice of mowers available is huge and the type that you buy will depend on the quality and size of the lawn (see Choosing a Mower, pages 49–53).

> **TIP** As with all tools and equipment, it is important that they are used safely and only for the jobs for which they are intended. The mains supply to electrical garden tools should be fitted with a circuit breaker, or RCD (residual current device), with a trip rating of 30 milliamps, to prevent accidental shock. If necessary, wear eye protection and gloves – and always wear sturdy boots!

Long-armed edging shears Used to trim the edges of the lawn to maintain a neat appearance. Hand shears could be used, but the long-armed types make a better job and prevent you having to bend. To cut cleanly, the shears should be kept clean and sharpened occasionally.

Wire rake Sometimes called a springbok or spring-tines rake. It has many uses around the garden, especially on the lawn, where it can be used to rake up leaves, twigs and other debris, for the removal of dead moss and thatch, and to lightly rake or groom the grass prior to mowing.

A cylinder mower, wire rake, long-armed edging shears and garden fork

A watering can and half moon edging iron

Half moon edging iron So called because of the shape of the blade. This semi-circular edging iron is used to cut a new edge along a bed or border and for turf repairs where you want to cut out a piece of turf. A spade could be used as a substitute, but they usually have a slightly curved blade and are not as easy to use as a half moon.

Watering can Very handy for applying weedkiller, moss killer and liquid fertilizer to the lawn. Ideally, you should keep a separate can solely for use on the lawn, as residues of selective weed killer can damage other plants, even if you wash out the watering can after use.

From top to bottom: an electric scarifyer, a push spiker, a thatch-removing rake and a hollow tine fork

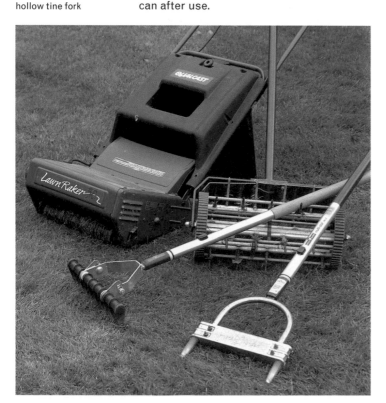

Other Items of Lawn Care Equipment

There are many other tools and pieces of equipment that make maintaining a lawn much easier, and if you intend to carry out seasonal lawn care it is well worth buying the ones that apply to you.

Scarifyer Sometimes called an electric lawn rake. They come in several sizes to suit all lawns and are well worth buying. Some models have a collector box; with others, you have to rake up manually afterwards. Professional petrol models are also available, but they are very expensive to buy. They can, however, be rented from specialist hire shops.

Thatch-removing rake This differs from a garden rake or wire rake in that the teeth are curved and sharp. As you pull the rake, the tines dig into the lawn and cut through dead moss, thatch and long stems. Very useful for ripping out old material in the base of the lawn and for loosening the surface soil wherever you want to carry out repairs to the lawn.

Hollow tine fork These are available in various designs, but all work the same. The hollow tines are pushed into the lawn and remove a core of soil. When they are pushed in the second time, the core of soil is forced out the top of the hollow tine by another soil core. To work well they must be kept clean and rust-free. For very large areas it is also possible to hire petrol hollow tine machines.

Push spiker Various solid tine spikes on a roller or board can be bought for aerating the lawn. The steel spikes vary from 5–10cm (2–4in) in length and are pushed into the surface of the lawn. Although this type of spike does not penetrate the ground as deeply as a garden fork, it is an ideal way of

Lawns

72

A strimmer, fertilizer spreader and hose-end feeder

walls and fences is also dealt with very quickly with a strimmer. For garden use, electric models are the most popular, although lightweight petrol models are perfect in large gardens where it is difficult to get an electricity supply. Some models can also be used to trim the edges of a lawn by altering the angle of the cutting head. With practice, you can get a reasonably neat finish, but many gardeners still prefer to use long-armed shears for the job.

Garden vacuum/blower This is another piece of equipment that more and more people are buying and on a lawn it is very useful for collecting fallen leaves in the autumn. Several models have a built in shredder which shreds the leaves as they are sucked up the tube into the collection bag. This allows more leaves to be collected between emptying the bag and it also means they will decompose faster when added to the compost heap. Some types also have a blow as well as sucking action and this is very useful for blowing large areas of leaves into a heap before collecting them. The blower can also be used to blow grass clippings off paths and drives after moving.

aerating a large area of lawn quickly and when used on a regular basis it greatly improves both surface drainage and aeration.

Fertilizer spreader Fertilizer can be spread by hand, but for an even distribution a spreader is much better, as when used properly the fertilizer is applied evenly across the area. Various designs are available (see Feeding, pages 54–7) to suit both small and large lawns. Most spreaders are made from strong plastic, making them light and easy to use, and many fertilizer manufacturers also make a spread designed for their own products. As well as fertilizer, you can apply weed and feed, moss killer and even grass seed through the spreader.

Strimmer Although not essential, a strimmer is a very useful tool to have in your garden shed. The spinning nylon cord is ideal for cutting long grass around trees and shrubs planted in the lawn, but you do need to be careful not to damage the bark on young plants. Long grass along the base of

An electric leaf blower

Hose pipe and sprinkler If you intend to water your lawn in periods of dry weather, you will need a hose pipe and sprinkler. Always buy a good quality hose that does not kink and for ease of use also buy a reel to wind the hose onto after use. A sprinkler will save you the time of having to stand with the hose and it will also distribute the water more evenly. Various types are available that can be adjusted to water different shapes and areas. Some even have a built in timer so that you can set the sprinkler to water for a set duration.

The most important time to water is when a lawn is establishing from seed or turf and this is where a good hose and sprinkler is very important. Check with your local water authority in case they have any rules or bylaws concerning the use of hose pipes and sprinklers.

Brush/besom A stiff sweeping brush or besom broom are ideal for working top dressing into the surface of the lawn, sweeping away worm casts and other debris and for dispersing dew on damp mornings prior to mowing.

Hose pipe stored on a reel with sprinkler attachment

Besom broom and turf float

Turf float This is a piece of equipment that is mainly used by greenkeepers, but if you intend to carry out lots of alterations to an existing lawn it is well worth looking out for. It is used to lift turf which has first been cut to shape with a half moon. The heart-shaped flat blade slices through the soil cutting the turf approximately 2.5–5cm (1–2in) thick. With practice, you can easily cut turf of an even thickness that can be re-laid elsewhere in the garden. Petrol turf lifters are also available for hire, for wherever you need to lift large areas of turf.

Turf box This is a simple piece of home-made equipment that is very useful if you are lifting turf by hand. It can be made easily by using a piece of strong plywood as the base with three raised wooden sides approximately 5cm (2in) deep. When the turf has been lifted, it is placed grass down in the tray and, using an old saw blade or old

scythe blade, any spare soil can be trimmed off by using the raised sides as a guide. It is a simple but effective way of making sure all the turves are the same thickness before they are re-laid (see Lawn Repairs, page 83).

Sieve If you plan to mix your own top dressing by using garden soil and sharp sand, a sieve will remove stones that might otherwise damage the mower. Choose a sieve with a mesh of 6mm (¼in). A larger meshed sieve can also be used for removing large stones from small, stony areas of the garden before sowing grass seed. For this type of work a sieve with a mesh of 12–25mm (½–1in) is ideal.

String line/wooden board A tight string line can be used to mark out a new lawn, paths or borders and is useful to mark the outer perimeter of a new lawn when laying turf or sowing seed. A wooden board is also useful when laying turf to prevent standing directly on the soil or newly laid turf. It can also be used when you want to re-edge a part of the lawn as it forms a solid guide for the half moon.

Roller Rolling a lawn should be kept to a minimum and is normally only done in spring as a result of heavy frosts lifting the surface of the lawn or on a newly laid lawn before the first cut. Even then only a light rolling is needed as heavy rolling can cause more problems by compacting the surface of the lawn. If your mower has a roller on it then there is no need to have a separate roller.

From left to right, a wooden board, string line and pegs, turf box and sieve

A roller can help keep a lawn looking its best, but should never be overused

Lawn Care Calendar

To keep your lawn in prime condition, there are certain jobs that need to be done at particular times of the year. All the various essential tasks are covered in other parts of this book, but have been brought together here to provide you with a quick-reference seasonal guide. However, the fact that all lawn maintenance have been included here does not mean that all these tasks must be undertaken every year. In many cases you will be able to get away with just doing the basic jobs such as mowing, feeding and weeding, but occasionally you will need to do a little extra work to the lawn in order to keep it healthy and looking its best.

The benefit of proper lawn care and maintenance is a lawn that will look good all year round. It will also be strong and healthy and less prone to attack from turf diseases, as well as able to withstand more wear and tear from pets and children.

The advent of spring marks a busy time in terms of lawn maintenance

Spring

Lawn maintenance starts in early spring when new growth is seen on the lawn. The first thing that is normally done is mowing, which should only be carried out on a dry day.

Early spring
- **Remove debris** Before you mow, pick up any twigs or branches that have accumulated on the lawn.
- **Rake over** Lightly rake over the lawn with a wire rake to lift any grasses that have laid flat over winter.
- **First mow** Mow with the blades set high so that the grass is just topped. Avoid mowing the lawn if heavy frosts are forecast.
- **Lightly roll** Gently firm the lawn surface down with a light roll, passing over just once. Do not use a heavy roller as this will cause surface compaction.
- **Moss control** Apply lawn sand or a proprietary moss killer as per instructions; Ferrous Sulphate in the product will also have a greening-up effect on the grass.

Early to mid-spring
- **Repairs** Carry out any repairs or restoration work in early to mid-spring: lay new turf and repair worn patches with turf lifted from the edge of the lawn.
- **Edges** Straighten up edges with a half moon edging iron to create a definite edge for easier trimming later on.
- **Over-seeding** Where grass cover is thin over-seed with a suitable seed mix.
- **Increase mowing** Gradually increase the mowing frequency and lower the blade until you reach desired height of cut.

Mid- to late spring
- **Diseases** Look out for diseases, especially if the weather is warm and

In early summer your lawn should be at its absolute peak

damp, and take remedial action as necessary (see Pests & Diseases, pages 136–40).

- **Scarifying** If you did not scarify in autumn it can be done in two directions; otherwise one pass should be enough to remove any dead moss and thatch.
- **Spiking** Any wet patches in the lawn can be spiked with a garden fork to help with aeration and surface drainage.
- **Feeding** Give the lawn its first feed of the season when the grass is actively growing and the weather is warmer. Apply either simple fertilizer, weed and feed or combined weed, feed and mosskiller. Do not use a high nitrogen fertilizer too early in the growing season, as this encourages soft, lush growth that is more prone to disease.
- **Weeding** Spray with a selective lawn weedkiller in late spring and feed a couple of weeks prior to using a weed-killer so that weeds are growing strongly with a larger leaf area to absorb the chemical.

Summer

During early summer, especially, lawns should be at their peak of condition. This is the time to enjoy your lawn to its fullest!

Early summer

- **Mow twice a week** This may seem a chore, but the grass will be in full growth and mowing little and often saves time in the long run and benefits the lawn greatly.
- **Scarify** Lightly scarify or rake the lawn to help control invasive grasses and to prevent thatch accumulating (do not carry this out in drought).
- **Water repairs** Areas of the lawn where repairs were carried out by turning or

seeding in spring will need watering if the soil is dry.
- **Continue weed control** Weed treatment can also be carried out if previous treatments have not killed all the weeds.
- **Trim edges** Keep lawn edges trimmed on a regular basis; if done little and often there are fewer clippings to collect.

Mid- to late summer

- **Reduce mowing** As temperatures rise and the ground starts to dry out, the grass usually slows down and you can reduce mowing frequency, raising the height of cut slightly.
- **Liquid feed** As growth slows, feed the lawn with a liquid feed that acts as an immediate tonic to help keep the grass green in these hotter months.
- **Irrigation** Water the lawn if needed in periods of drought when the grass shows signs of drying out. Lightly prick over the area to help the water to soak into the soil.
- **Weed control** Late summer is the last chance to control weeds.
- **Fertilizer** Late summer is the last time to apply a summer fertilizer before growth starts to slow.

Autumn

The busiest time in the lawn care calendar, a little work carried out in the autumn will vastly improve your lawn for the following year.

- **First rains** Wait till the first autumn rains soften the ground; otherwise, jobs will be difficult to carry out and you risk damaging the lawn.
- **Fertilizer** If you do no other maintenance, apply an autumn fertilizer to stimulate root growth and encourage winter hardiness and disease resistance.
- **Collect leaves** As the first autumn leaves fall collect on a regular basis – at least once a week.
- **Moss control** Cool, damp autumn sees the return of moss and you will need to apply a mosskiller to control it. Once it has turned black, rake it out by hand or with a mechanical scarifyer.
- **Worm casts** Worms can be a problem, especially on close mown fine lawns. Wait for them to dry on a fine day and sweep them off with a stiff brush.
- **Spiking and top dressing** Carry out spiking with either solid or hollow tines. If hollow tining, follow with a top dressing well brushed into the surface of the lawn.
- **Over-seeding** Thin patches can be over-seeded with a suitable mixture. The seed should germinate quickly in moist conditions and will normally establish before the onset of winter.
- **Check for diseases** Look out for patches of yellow or distressed grass, especially if the autumn weather is mild and wet. Chemical control is difficult, but some diseases can be controlled by cultural methods such as brushing and good aeration.
- **Swish!** Brushing, or 'swishing', the lawn occasionally to disperse morning dew is beneficial during autumn. This helps prevent fungal diseases.
- **Lay/sow a new lawn** Autumn is also the ideal time to lay turf or sow grass seed, be it a new lawn or repairs to an existing one.

Autumn is the time to put in the work that will benefit your lawn for the rest of the year

The amount of work you will be able to do on your lawn in winter depends on the prevailing weather conditions

Winter

Although grass growth slows down during the winter months, there are still several jobs to do. As long as the lawn is not waterlogged or frozen, it can still be used and enjoyed.

- **Brush leaves** Rake or brush off the last of the autumn leaves; this will also help to disperse dew and worm casts.
- **Mowing** Cut on a dry day if the grass is still growing, but lift the height of cut so that the grass is just topped.
- **Check for diseases** Early winter is the time when several diseases strike, so look out for dead patches or areas where the grass is discoloured.
- **Turf repairs** It is too late in most areas to sow seed, but turf can be laid without any problems. You can also work on damaged edges and lift or lower turf where there are hollows or humps.
- **New lawn** Lightly trim autumn-sown grass seed or newly laid turf to encourage the sward to thicken up.
- **Maintain drainage** Aerate by spiking as and when needed to keep the surface of the lawn well-drained. If puddles remain, it might be worth digging a soak away or installing a simple drain (see Drainage, pages 22–4).
- **Service tools and equipment** When the grass eventually stops growing, clean and service mowers, tools and equipment ready for next year.
- **Avoid frost damage** Keep off the lawn in periods of heavy frost. Damage will show as yellow foot-prints a few days after the frost has thawed.

Avoid walking on frost- or snow-covered lawns which can be easily damaged

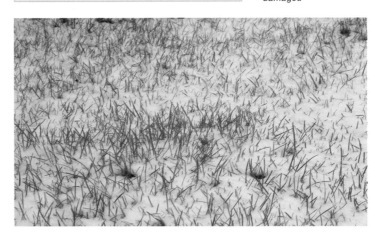

Care of Mowers & Equipment

Most tools and pieces of equipment used on the lawn will last for many years as long as a small amount of routine maintenance is carried out. In most cases it is simply a case of keeping them clean and free from soil and wet grass clippings, which can be corrosive to metal. With mowers, a little more work may be required, especially at the end of the cutting season, but this is well worth doing, as it prolongs the life of the mower and makes cutting more efficient.

Maintaining Hand Tools

Keeping tools clean and free from rust is the main aim and this can be done very easily. If the metal is clean, the tool is much easier to

It is worth keeping tools clean and rust-free, as they will perform better if cared for properly

use. A rusty half moon or fork is difficult to use and will not make as neat a job.

After using the tool any soil sticking to them should be washed off. This might mean using a hose pipe and brush if you have been working in heavy clay soil, although on light sandy soil you should be able to brush the loose soil off easily.

If the tools are made of stainless steel, which does not rust, they can be dried with an old cloth and put away until they are needed again.

Steel tools

Steel-bladed tools, however, do rust and you need to take precautions to prevent it from forming. Once the tools have been washed

TIP

Clean tools by plunging them into a bucket of sharp sand to which a small amount of oil has been added. The sand removes loose soil and coats the steel with protective oil.

If your tools have rusted, a wire brush and some oil will often solve the problem

Sharpening tools

If your shears do not cut very well, it may be that the centre nut has come loose and needs to be tightened slightly. If this does not solve the problem they may need sharpening. Use a metal file or small grinder to sharpen along the edge of the blade, making sure that you follow the line of the original bevel on the blade.

Alternatively, you can take them to your local mower or hardware shop where they can sharpen them for you.

and the metal work is dry, apply a small amount of oil to the metal work and wipe over with a cloth. This thin film of oil will prevent rust from forming.

Handles

The handles of many tools are made from plastic coated alloy or plastic and these simply need wiping down with a damp cloth to remove soil. If the handles and shafts are wooden, it is a good idea to wipe them down occasionally with a cloth dipped in linseed. This helps to keep the wood supple and prevents it from splintering. Any moving parts should also be oiled, especially on hand shears and long-armed edging shears, once they have been wiped clean.

Maintaining Mowers & Electrical Equipment

Maintenance of modern mowers is very simple and many electric mowers and other pieces of electrical equipment such as strimmers and scarifiers need very little attention. As long as they are kept clean and protected against corrosion, there is little else to do. Petrol mowers do require a little more attention and this can either be done at home or by a mower workshop.

Electric mowers

The electric motors on mowers and other pieces of garden equipment are sealed units and require no maintenance. When they break it is usually cheaper to buy a new mower than to try and repair the old one.

> **TIP**
> Always disconnect electrical equipment from the mains supply before carrying out any cleaning or maintenance. Never use a hose pipe to wash down electrical equipment.

Clean the pan of your electric mower after every cut to ensure optimum performance

Maintenance mainly consists of keeping the mower clean after use. Grass clippings that have accumulated underneath the mower should be scraped off and the mower given a quick wipe down. If clippings are allowed to build up, not only does it put more strain on the mower, but the grass will not be cut or collected as efficiently.

At the end of the season after cleaning check the blade and sharpen or replace if necessary. Some of the smaller types have a small plastic disposable blade that is very easy to replace when worn.

Petrol mowers

Petrol engines do need to be checked regularly to keep them working in good order. An instruction manual should be supplied with the mower which will have

Most petrol mowers now run on unleaded fuel

Adjusting the cylinder

In order to cut grass cleanly the cylinder needs to be properly adjusted onto the fixed bottom blade. Test the cut by holding a piece of paper between the bottom blade and cylinder; when the blade is turned by hand the paper should be cut cleanly. If the blades turn freely and the paper passes between the cylinder and bottom blade you will need to adjust the blade down. This is normally done by tightening a screw or small bolt at each end of the cylinder.

details of lubricants, fuel type and servicing requirements.

During the mowing season, maintenance mainly involves checking the oil level and keeping the machine clean. With two-stroke engines you need to pay particular attention to the correct petrol and oil mix. If too little oil is used in the mixture, the engine will wear faster and if too much oil is used it will smoke excessively.

After mowing, any loose grass clippings should be brushed off to prevent them from building up into a thick layer. With rotary mowers this will mean tipping the mower on one side to scrape off the wet

Check the oil level in the sump of your petrol mower before every cut

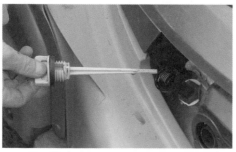

Mower air filters clog rapidly with grass clippings and other debris, so clean them regularly

TIP
Before working on any petrol engine, always remove the spark plug cover to prevent the engine starting accidentally.

clippings – details of which way to tilt the mower are normally given in the instruction manual. The blade may also need checking if an obstruction such as a stone or stick has been mown over.

Servicing a petrol mower

Petrol mowers do need a basic service in the winter at the end of the mowing season. This can normally be carried out at home, but when a more detailed repair is needed, use a mower specialist. Check the following:

- Drain the petrol tank and put in fresh fuel
- Change the oil
- Clean the spark plug
- Check the air filter
- Oil moving parts
- Sharpen blades

Check the spark plug and periodically clean it with wire wool in order to maintain best performance

Renovating Lawns

Very often when you move to a different property, you inherit an old, neglected lawn. You then must decide whether to start from scratch and lay a new lawn from turf or seed, or to renovate the existing lawn.

If the overall standard of the lawn is fairly good and there is a reasonable covering of grass, then it is worth renovating. Weeds, moss, patchy growth, small hollows and high spots can all be dealt with without too many problems.

You also need to consider the amount of work involved in removing the old lawn, preparing the soil and re-laying a new lawn and, of course, the cost that this will entail. Although there will be some work involved in renovating a neglected lawn, it is well worth the effort. As long as there is a basic lawn to start with, you should be able to transform it into a good quality lawn within one season of growth.

Initial Improvements

Regular mowing will greatly improve an area of grass that has been neglected and if the lawn is very long, the first thing to do is cut the grass. This may involve the use of a petrol strimmer initially, to get the grass down to a manageable height. Once the long grass has been raked off, you can mow again with a rotary mower and gradually reduce the height of cut. To start with the lawn will look as though it has been scalped, but new growth will soon be made and the lawn will green up. This initial renovation can be done any time during the growing season, but avoid mowing the grass too short in dry weather unless you are able to water.

If you start work in the spring you can also feed the lawn, and treat for weeds and moss once it has been mown several times

and recovered from the initial mowing. Throughout the summer, continue to weed and feed and mow on a regular basis. If you are starting in the autumn, carry out moss control and apply an autumn lawn feed to strengthen the grass over winter.

Making Repairs

Once the grass is growing and you have made a start on weed and moss control, you can then begin the serious work of renovating the lawn. The best time to make repairs is during the autumn and spring.

You may also need to carry out other maintenance tasks that have been described earlier in the book such as spiking, scarification, top-dressing and over-seeding in order to help improve the quality of the lawn.

Lifting turf

On occasion, you may need a small quantity of turf to carry out repairs or to extend the lawn. Buying in new turf is one option, but if the existing lawn is old and well established the new turf may stand out against the old when laid due to the different grass mixture. One way of overcoming this is to lift some of your own turf, and by widening a border slightly, you can often gain enough turf to carry out the extra work.

Turf is most easily lifted by using a turf float, which is specially designed for the job

To lift turf you can get a special tool called a turf float which has a heart-shaped flat blade and long handle. However, unless you intend to lift turf on a regular basis, a spade will do just as well. Use a half moon to make the vertical cuts and slide the spade under the grass to a depth of at least 2.5cm (1in). With a little practice you will be able to lift the turf to an even thickness that is suitable for re-laying.

Patching with turf

There are two ways that you can repair bare patches on a lawn – turf and seed. When patching with turf try to use pieces from the same lawn as new turf will look different. The best time to carry out turf repairs is in spring or autumn, although they can be done at most times of the year as long as the new turf can be watered in dry weather.

1 – Using a half-moon, cut out a square of turf around the damaged area and lift the turf with a spade or turf float.

2 – Lightly fork the exposed soil to loosen it, rake it level and gently re-firm to create a level surface for the roots to grow into.

3 – Cut turf from another part of the lawn. Check that the turf is level with the surrounding grass and firm it down before watering.

Patching with seed

If there are too many patches to turf, seed is an excellent alternative option, as it is a fast and inexpensive method of replacement.

For lawns where there are too many bare patches to turf, or where you are unable to lift some of your own turf, patching with seed is another option. Ideally, this should be done in early autumn and spring, the two times of the year when grass seed germinates and establishes quickly.

1 – Using a small fork or rake, loosen the soil on the bare patches, rake it level and firm the area to create a seed bed to sow onto.

2 – Sprinkle grass seed over the bare patch by hand.

3 – Lightly work the seed by hand into the surface of the soil. Cover over the newly-seeded area with a piece of garden fleece, pegged down to prevent it from blowing away. This will protect the seed from birds and also prevent the surface drying out too quickly. Once the grass has grown through, the fleece can be removed.

TIP

To prevent a patchy appearance, try to choose a seed mixture that has similar characteristics to the original lawn. When seeding bare patches, ideally over-seed the whole lawn for a more uniform appearance.

Pre-chitting the seed

Grass seed can be pre-chitted, where seed is allowed to start the germination process before it is sown for faster establishment. To chit the seed, add two or three handfuls of grass seed to a bucket of moist compost (multi-purpose or potting) and mix them together. Stand the bucket in a warm place and check the seed after a few days. As soon as the seed starts to produce small shoots, sow over the bare patch that has been forked over and levelled. Take a handful of the seed and compost mixture and spread thinly over the area.

Humps & hollows

To make mowing as easy as possible the lawn should be on a reasonably level plane. Gradual undulations are fine as the mower will simply follow the contours, but small humps and hollows not only make mowing more difficult, they look unsightly. The hollows are difficult to mow because the mower rides over them and they also attract standing water after periods of heavy rain. Humps are often scalped as the mower passes over them and in extreme cases the grass is sliced off to expose the soil below.

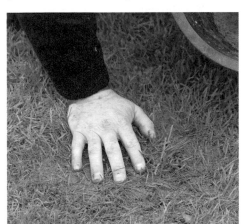

Systematically applying layers of top dressing is one way of sorting out minor hollows in lawns

Raising with top dressing Shallow depressions can be built up over a period of time by applying top dressing which is worked into the grass. However, it is important not to smother the grass with the top dressing. As the grass grows, another dressing can be applied until the hollow is level with the surrounding lawn. This method is effective where you only need to raise the level slightly, but for deeper hollows the best way to deal with them is to lift the turf and in-fill with fresh soil.

Cutting and filling beneath turf

1 – To repair a deeper hollow in a lawn, cut a cross in the lawn over the hollow, slice under the turf and fold it back neatly. Ideally the cross should extend wider than the hollow so that when the turf is folded back it reveals the depressions and some of the level ground around it.

2 – Add some garden soil to the hollow. Spread it around evenly with your hands, or if necessary use a rake. Firm the added soil until it is level with the surrounding soil.

3 – Fold the turf back into its original position and firm down, pressing the cut seams of turf tightly together.

The procedure for dealing with a hump is exactly the same , but instead of adding soil, you need to remove some of the existing soil to reduce the level of the protusion.

1

2

3

Repairing damaged edges

Lawn edges can be damaged very easily by a mower slipping off the lawn into the border. Similarly, if you walk too close to the edge of the border as you mow, you will cause damage. Broken edges should always be repaired as soon as possible before the damaged area gets larger. Building up a crumbing edge is very difficult as there is nothing to hold the soil back, so the best approach is to create a solid new edge with turf.

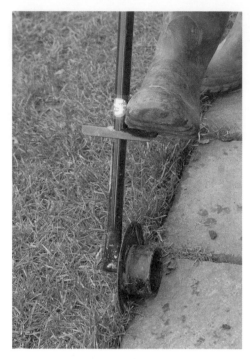

This neat cutting wheel offers the easiest solution for tidying edges along solid paths

1

2

3

4

1 – Cut out a square of turf around the damaged edge using a half-moon edging iron. Make the cut to a depth of at least 2.5cm (1in).

2 – Lift the turf using a turf float or ordinary spade, ensuring that the cut you make is as even as possible.

3 – Reverse the square of turf so that a new edge is formed along the border and the damaged area is now set back into the lawn.

4 – The hole can either be patched in with a small piece of turf, or it can be filled with soil and seeded. In most cases, the neatest solution will be to cut a small patch of turf from a hidden corner of grass.

> **TIP**
>
> To maintain a neat edge where grass grows up to a path or driveway, a half moon can be used very easily as you just follow the line of the paving. Alternatively, there are products available for edging that have a cutting wheel that trim the edge when pushed along.

Maintaining path edges

Over a period of time grass will creep sideways onto a path, and if allowed to carry on doing this it will eventually reduce the width of the path. It also creates an untidy appearance, because there is no definite edge to the path.

Where the grass has been allowed to grow over the edge for a few years you will need to cut back to the original path line with a half moon and then scrape off the paving. You can also use a half moon to create a definite edge where grass grows up to a gravel path. It is worth the effort involved in keeping the edges of paths looking neat and tidy.

Use a half moon edging iron for tidying path edges when the medium used in the path is not solid

Strengthening worn areas

There are always going to be areas of the lawn that are used more than others and as a result worn patches may appear. As already mentioned, these can be repaired by seeding or turfing, but if they are areas that are used as a path across the lawn, the repair will only be a temporary measure. One remedy would be to remove the affected part of the lawn and build a path, but if you want to keep the area down to grass then you need to look at reinforcing the area.

There are several products available that can be used to strengthen areas of a lawn that are exposed to heavy foot use or even light vehicular traffic. Some of the heavier types need to be installed before the lawn is laid, but the products suitable for garden use can usually be laid on an established lawn.

Laying mesh First, mow the grass as short as possible to start with and then brush in a top dressing of sharp sand to fill in any minor undulations and create a firm, level surface. The reinforcing mesh can then be laid out over the area. Some types are sectional and clip together and others are supplied in a roll. Peg down the mesh and brush a thin layer of sand over the area. The grass will then grow through the mesh and

Plastic reinforcing mesh can be bought from any good garden centre

Dealing with border plants

Plants growing in beds and borders can also cause problems to the edge of a lawn. As the plants grow and spread they often grow out over the lawn and eventually kill the grass by blocking out light. Pruning back the plants is one answer, but this is only a temporary measure, because the shrubs will soon grow back again over the lawn. Widening the border is the best solution, as it not only creates a new edge to the lawn, but the plants will be able to grow naturally.

When using a reinforcing mesh in your lawn it is better if the grass is not mown too short, as this may expose the mesh. Mowing and feeding is done as normal, although you will not be able to carry out scarification or spiking, as this might damage the mesh.

after a short while the roots will grow around the mesh to form a strong base.

This type of reinforcing is ideal for grass paths that need to be used all year round and for places where you occasionally want to drive a car. Not only does the mesh reduce grass wear, it also stabilizes the top soil and prevents soil erosion, making it ideal for use on slopes as well as flat ground.

Cutting Out Tree Roots

The roots of trees and shrubs can be a problem on old lawns where they have grown very close to the surface. The roots can make mowing more difficult and where they are pronounced they can damage the

Cut offending roots as deeply into the lawn as possible, using a pair of secateurs

mower. Suckering shoots growing from the roots can also be a nuisance and although regular mowing will cut them off, if they have not been chopped off on a regular basis and are woody at their base, they also can damage the mower, especially if it is a cylinder type.

The only way to deal with these roots is to peel back the turf around them and cut them off, preferably back into the border where they will do no harm.

Very thick roots on large established trees are a little more difficult to cut out completely and in this situation you may be able to remove an area of turf, build up the soil slightly and then re-turf the affected area. This will create a slight mound in the lawn, but at least the root will be out of harm's way.

Use a spade to lift roots that are coming to the surface of the lawn

Tree bases

Mowing can be difficult around the base of established and newly planted trees growing in a lawn. Because you cannot get right up to the tree with the mower, you are left with clump of long grass that has to be cut down with a strimmer or pair of shears. By removing a circle of grass from around the base of the tree, it not only makes mowing much easier, it also looks neater. In the case of young trees, an area of bare soil at the base of the tree will help growth, because the water and nutrients will be able to get down to the tree roots instead of being robbed by the grass.

Compost Lawn Clippings

Over a growing season a lawn will generate a large amount of grass clippings – in fact, it is estimated that a 100sq m (100sq yd) lawn produces over 100kg (440lb) of clippings in a season, depending on the type of grass and growing conditions. This represents quite a large pile of clippings that needs to be disposed of. Fortunately, grass clippings soon break down, and they can be added to a compost bin or compost heap. As grass clippings mainly consist of water, when you try to compost them on their own the result is often a black, slimy mess that is of no use. However, there are products available that can be mixed with the clippings to help turn them into useable garden compost, but for the best results they should be mixed with other garden waste such as prunings, vegetable waste, leaves and weeds and added to a compost bin. The grass clippings will retain moisture in the heap and help the contents to heat up, which is essential for the decomposition process.

Fresh grass clippings are also used by many gardeners as a mulch spread 3–4cm (1½in) thick around established trees and shrubs in borders, or around the base of fruit trees. They will help to retain moisture, reduce weed growth and add some nutrients back into the soil.

Put grass clippings into a compost bin or heap, but always mix them with other matter to create decent compost

OTHER LAWN FEATURES

In many gardens the lawn is the central feature – the first thing you see when entering the garden – and for this reason it might be worth creating something a little different to add a unique appearance to the lawn. By mowing in different directions or by creating mowing stripes in patterns you can make the lawn look much more interesting – and of course if you are not happy with the results, you simply mow them out!

TIP

It is also possible to mow with a roller and leave no stripe. To do this you mow up and down the same strip before moving across to mow the second strip. This method is slower because you have to mow each strip twice, but the result is a lawn free from stripes.

Mowing Patterns

A stripe on the lawn looks good and brings a professional quality to your mowing

Lawns need to be mown on a regular basis to keep them healthy and looking good. Usually, this consists of mowing up and down or round and round, depending on the shape and size of the lawn.

Creating stripes

To mow stripes on the lawn you need a mower with a roller. It does not matter whether it is a cylinder or rotary mower, as it is the roller that creates the stripe by bending the grass over in one direction. To create stripes you simply mow one strip up the lawn, turn around and mow back down, and so on; this will create light and dark stripes. When you look at the light and dark

Lawns

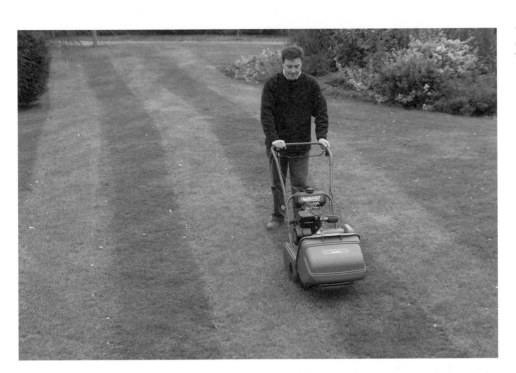

The wider the mower's rear roller, the broader the stripe you will create

green stripes on a newly mown lawn, it is the light coloured stripes that go away from you and the dark ones that come towards you, due to the manner in which the roller bends the blades of grass downwards.

On many lawns the stripes look best if they are applied in straight lines, but where you have shaped borders, you can follow the curves to create flowing, contoured stripes across the lawn. This effect will lead your eye around the garden and create a very informal and relaxed feel to the lawn.

Broad stripes To give the effect of broad stripes, as you would see on a football field, mow two or three stripes next to each other in one direction followed by the same number in the opposite direction. It takes a little more thinking about setting out the first time you mow this way, in order to make sure that the spacing of the stripes is correct, but once applied the stripes will be there to follow the next time you mow.

Cross stripes To create a cross-striped effect, mow as usual in one direction and then mow the lawn again at right angles, crossing the first line of stripes.

TIP

Dragging a mat or wide brush over the lawn will also create a stripe, so if in the winter you want to stripe your lawn but it does not need cutting, simply walk up and down dragging a mat to form stripes. This also disperses the dew at the same time.

Criss-cross patterns are more elaborate and provide a talking point

Mowing at Different Levels

Allowing the grass to grow at different levels within the lawn will provide contrasting textures and colours and you can also create some interesting mowing patterns by altering the height of cut. These can be very simple designs or intricate geometric patterns and can be applied on lawns of all sizes, but the larger the lawn, the more ambitious you can be.

Close-mown shapes

The best way to create the designs is to wait until the lawn is ready for mowing and then mark out the pattern with garden canes pushed into the ground. You can use string, but it tends to get in the way. When you are happy with the shape, mow quite close so that it stands out from the surrounding grass. The remainder of the lawn can then be lightly topped or you can leave it to carry on growing. For this type of mown pattern to work there needs to be a minimum of 25mm (1in) difference between the grass heights.

Mown shapes look great but must be cut deep enough to be effective

Mowing paths

Close mown paths that run through a large lawn are another device that can add interest, and they also serve a purpose by indicating where you should and should not walk. The mown path can also be used to link two areas of the garden together. For example, if you have a closely mown area of the garden and another area of longer grass where the children play, or perhaps a small orchard, a mown path will lead you from one area to another.

The larger the area, the longer you can allow the grass to grow at the side of the lawn to create a natural effect. Avoid letting the grass grow too long at the side of a mown path in a very small garden, as this can make the garden look unkempt.

TIP

When you are mowing patterns or shapes at different cutting heights in your lawn, start by mowing the entire area on the high setting and then mow the shorter parts. This gives a much neater finish than doing it the other way round.

A mown grass path helps direct traffic across the garden and makes an interesting visual feature. However, the path must be cut deep enough to be noticed!

Mowing spirals and mazes

Mowing a spiral in a lawn is a very fast and simple way of adding some humour to the garden. Small children will love walking around the spiral to the centre.

Start mowing at the centre point and mow outwards in a spiral shape. The method is quite simple to pick up once you get started, as long as you leave an even gap of un-mown grass between each circuit as you mow around the enlarging circle.

For something a little more ambitious, you could try mowing a simple maze into your lawn. This will take a little more setting out, but when it is finished it will give children and adults hours of fun – without the risk of getting lost! Draw the plan of your maze on paper first to avoid making errors once you have got the mower out.

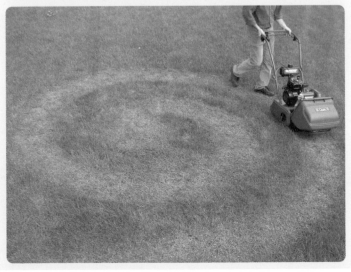

Bulbs in Lawns

Drifts of flowering bulbs can look stunning in a lawn, but they are not practical in all situations. After flowering the foliage has to be allowed to die down naturally, and this can take several weeks, which means that the grass around the clumps of bulbs can grow very long. On a large lawn or in areas where it does not matter if the grass grows longer – such as an orchard, a meadow, around the base of trees or a grassy bank – this is fine, but on a small closely mown area, it might cause problems. One way around this is to use early flowering bulbs such as crocus, snowdrops (Galanthus) and early daffodils (Narcissus) where the foliage dies down before the main mowing season starts.

Planting Bulbs

When buying bulbs to naturalize in the lawn, always buy good quality ones. Very often small, cheaper bulbs are sold for planting in lawns, but you will get a better display if you go for the large ones. The bulbs should be firm and not showing any signs of mould or rot. Plant bulbs when the soil is moist, as dry soil is much more difficult to plant into.

Ideally, plant the bulbs to at least twice their depth. For example, a bulb measuring 5cm (2in) should be planted so that there is 10cm (4in) of soil above the top of the bulb. Not only will planting at this depth ensure that the bulbs establish well, but the depth of soil around the growing leaves and flower stalk will help to support them in windy conditions. Bulbs planted too shallow often blow over very easily.

Large bulbs Plant larger bulbs, such as daffodils, with a spade. Simply chop several squares in the lawn with the spade and lift the soil, complete with turf. To make it easier, lift several squares at a time and then place several bulbs into each hole and

93

A bulb planter will make neat incisions in the lawn, into whch you simply place your bulbs

and snowdrops. However, because these tools only take out a core of soil approximately 10–15cm (4–6in) deep, you are limited as to the size of bulb that you can plant. However, for snowdrops, crocus and dwarf daffodils, bulb cutters are very effective.

Push the planter into the ground and remove a core of soil. Then place the bulbs into the hole and cover over with the soil core. Again, if the soil is clay, break it up a little before replacing it into the hole on top of the bulbs.

Aftercare

Once the bulbs start to push through the grass, care should be taken not to walk on them or mow over them.

Once they have finished flowering, the foliage should be allowed to die down naturally. This helps to build up the bulb for the following season and takes around six weeks. Only when the foliage is yellow and dying down can it be cut off.

Deadheading is also beneficial as the plant will divert its energy into building up the bulb rather than seed production.

You can use a lawn fertilizer where bulbs are planted – in fact it will help the bulbs to develop and multiply – but avoid using a feed and weed as this may damage the bulbs before they become established.

fold back the soil and turf and then firm with your foot. If the soil is heavy clay, try to break it up rather than covering the bulbs with a solid lump. This is a fast and efficient way of planting large numbers of bulbs in a lawn.

Smaller bulbs A bulb planter tool is ideal for planting smaller bulbs such as crocus

If you want to create a concentrated effect with several bulbs together, lift a larger chunk of turf

Wildflowers in the Lawn

Growing wildflowers in gardens is becoming very popular and a lawn provides the perfect place to grow many of them. The size of your garden and lawn will determine what you are able to grow, but even on a small lawn it is still possible to grow a few wildflowers and create a small piece of countryside in your own garden. Deciding what are wildflowers and what are lawn weeds is a matter for you to decide. In a formal lawn buttercups are classed as weeds, but in a wildflower meadow they look magnificent and should be encouraged.

Wildflowers are ideal where you want to create a natural area in the lawn and as well as looking attractive, you are also helping to conserve plant species that may be reducing in numbers in the natural habitat. This is also a very good way of attracting wildlife into the garden. Birds will feed on the seeds; butterflies, moths and insects will feed on the flowers; and small mammals and frogs will use the longer grass as a hiding place.

Plants suitable for a meadow

There are many wildflowers suitable for growing in a meadow, such as speedwell, buttercup, self-heal, field scabious, plantain, lady's bedstraw, bird's-foot trefoil, hawkbit, clover, knapweed, ox-eye daisy and many more (see Broad-leaved Weeds and Wildflowers, pages 113–27). These are all perennial plants that can survive in grass land that is not mown closer than around 5cm (2in).

Meadow Lawns

Creating a meadow is best done where you have more than one lawn, as for much of the year the grass will be long and unsuitable for recreational activities. Alternatively, if you have a large lawn you may be able to create a meadow area at the top end of the lawn, with a path mown through the meadow to give access to other parts of the garden.

There are two ways of creating a meadow. One involves planting wildflowers into an established lawn and the other way is to sow a mixture of grass seed and wildflower seeds onto an area of bare earth.

Ox-eye daisies mix with plantains and geraniums to create a delightful meadow effect

Establishing a meadow from seed

Before sowing the wildflower mixture, the ground must be cleared of all perennial weeds such as docks and nettles in the same way that you would to create an ornamental lawn (see Preparing for a New Lawn, pages 25–7). Do not apply fertilizer, however, as low fertility is essential for the wildflowers to establish. Where the soil is very fertile the grasses will grow very quickly and swamp the small wildflower seedlings.

Many seed companies sell meadow mixes that contain a selection of grasses

TIP Low fertility is the order of the day in any wildflower meadow and under no circumstances should the area ever be fed with a lawn fertilizer. This is to prevent vigorous grass species smothering other plants; where soil nutrients are low, you will get better flowering wildflowers. Grass clippings should also be removed after every cut.

and perennial wildflowers. Sow these in mid-spring or early autumn onto a firm seed bed. The sowing rate is normally much less than when sowing for a lawn to prevent the plants becoming over-crowded – follow the supplier's instructions.

Aftercare – first season For the first growing season after sowing do not expect flowers; instead the aim is to establish the plants. When the sward reaches approximately 10cm (4in) top with a rotary mower, making sure all the grass clippings are removed. If they are left on to rot down, they will add nutrients back to the soil and encourage lush grass growth. Maintain the height of cut to around 10cm (4in) by mowing once a month and removing the clippings each time.

Aftercare – second season At the start of the second season, top the meadow area to tidy it up after the winter and then allow it to grow and develop. The wildflower will bloom from mid-spring through until the summer, and when all flowering has finished and the wildflowers have shed their seeds, carry out the second cut of the season. This is normally around late summer or early autumn, depending on the type of flowers in the meadow. The second cut is more difficult due to the length of growth and is best done with a petrol strimmer. Rake off the hay and give the area a final tidy up with a rotary mower and collection box.

Establishing a wildflower meadow from seed does take a few years and you do need

1

1 – Where you want to establish a wildflower meadow on a bare patch of garden, you can do it by sowing seed. Some companies sell a complete seed mixture or you can over-seed a newly sown plot with a wildflower seed mix. Sowing the wildflower seed separately gives the gardener more control of where the seed is being sown. Wildflower seed is very small and only needs to be sown thinly.

2

2 – To ensure the seed is distributed evenly over the area, it can be mixed with a quantity of light sand. Add the seed and sand into a bucket and mix the two thoroughly together before sowing the seed thinly over the prepared area.

3

3 – Once sown, the seed can be lightly raked into the soil surface. Germination can be slow and erratic. In fact, some types of wildflowers can take up to six months to germinate or in some cases they will only germinate in spring after they have been through a winter, so do not expect instant results.

Mini meadows

Even on small lawns it is possible to grow some wildflowers while still maintaining a neatly mown lawn. To create a mini meadow, mark out a small circle within the lawn that is going to be planted and set out a selection of perennial wildflowers that are suitable for growing in grass. Position the plants in small groups to give a mixture of colours and flowering heights and plant with a trowel or bulb planter. All the plants need to be well firmed into the soil and given a thorough watering and kept moist until they establish. Planting can be done in early spring or autumn.

After planting, the grass within the wildflower circle is not mown, but the lawn surrounding the small circle is mown and treated as normal. At the end of the flowering season the circle can be strimmed down and used as a lawn until the following spring, when the wildflowers are allowed to grow again.

to be patient. Many types of plants are slow to germinate and establish, and invasive weeds may be a problem in the early days needing spot treating with a suitable weedkiller to control them. After a few years when the fertility of the soil is reduced by the removal of all clippings, the growth will calm down and a balance of broad-leaved wildflowers and grasses will even out.

Planting a meadow

Where you already have an established lawn that you want to turn into a wildflower meadow, you can introduce perennial wildflowers by planting directly. This is a much faster way to establish a meadow and you will get flowers the first season after planting. Young plants are available from garden centres and specialist wildflower nurseries, or you can grow many types very easily from seed.

Planting can be done at most times of the year, but spring and autumn are the best times to introduce the plants. Plants growing in small pots can be planted with a trowel or a bulb planter that removes a core of soil. After planting, make sure the plants are well-firmed into the soil and watered in.

Spread larger plants around the lawn prior to planting them in order to ensure an even distribution

If the weather turns dry after planting, keep the young plants watered until they are properly established.

Maintenance is the same as that for seeds – an early spring cut and again in late summer when the wildflowers have seeded.

Daisy circles

Where you already have a heavy weed population such as daisies growing in your lawn, you can turn it to your advantage and create flowering circles or indeed any other shape to create an interesting feature. Growing wildflowers in this way can be easily achieved in any garden, no matter what the size of the lawn.

Simply mow around a group of broad-leaved weeds in spring to form the desired shape and allow them to grow and flower. Mow the remainder of the lawn as normal every week in order to create a neat finish – and at the same time you will get the wonderful effect of white daisy flowers tinged with pink that give a stunning natural display on a sunny day. When the daisies finish flowering in late spring, mow over the circles and carry out maintenance as usual along with the rest of the lawn. The daisies will continue to flourish in the lawn and will flower again the following spring.

TIP A wildflower circle can also be created with other spring flowering plants such as buttercups, clover and speedwell.

Aftercare

Growing wildflowers or weeds in lawns in this way does mean some small changes will be needed in how you carry out maintenance on your lawn.

Weedkillers For a start, lawn weedkillers will no longer be required, unless you intend to keep the areas outside the circle weed free. If this is the case, take care not to allow spray to drift into the wildflower areas.

Feeding It is not normally necessary to feed the plants, as they grow best when there is less competition from the grass. If you do use a lawn fertilizer, feed only the regularly mown areas of grass around the wildflower circles.

Mowing Mow around the circles as usual, but only when flowering is complete should the circles be mown down. A rotary mower set high is the best way to mow off the long grass, and thereafter you can mow the

A daisy circle can be as big or as small as you like, depending on the size of your lawn

Micro-clover

Micro-clover is a very low growing and spreading form of white clover that has been developed for use in lawns. In the past, white clover has been classed as a lawn weed, but this strain of clover is being included in some grass seed mixtures. The even spread of the plant does not create a patchy effect like other clovers, and because the leaves are tiny they do not dominate the grass species. Trials have shown that lawns that include micro-clover stay greener in dry weather and less nitrogenous fertilizer is needed due to the nitrogen fixing nodules on the roots. Although flowers are produced, the flowering period is short, and on regularly mown lawns the micro-clover flowers contain very little nectar and do not attract bees, which are often a worry when children play on lawns containing clover.

circle along with the remainder of the lawn. A cutting height of around 2.5cm (1in) is fine for most plants throughout the growing season.

Cornfield Annuals

These are brightly coloured summer flowering annuals such as field poppies, cornflower and corn marigold that people often associate with wildflower meadows, although they do not grow in permanent grass land. To grow they need cultivated land, hence the reason you see them growing in cornfields and other arable land. It is, however, possible to create a small area within an existing lawn where these annual wildflowers can be grown.

Simply remove a small patch of turf approximately 5cm (2in) thick and lightly

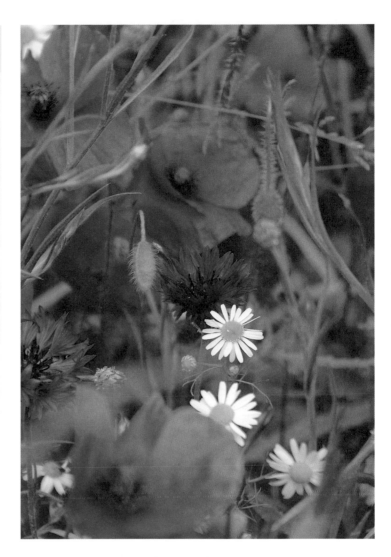

fork over the soil to create a seed bed. The seeds of these annual wildflowers are readily available and can be sown thinly over the area in autumn or early spring. Flowers will be produced during the summer and the plants will then die, but should be left to drop their seed over the soil. In late summer, rake over the soil to keep the surface loose and the following season you will get another crop of seedling plants.

Although, in theory, the cornfield annuals will seed themselves every year, sometimes one type of flower may become dominant, in which case you may have to sow some extra seeds of the other types to maintain a balance.

Poppies, cornflowers and mayweeds create fantastic natural colour combinations

Turf Sculptures

Grass is a very versatile plant which can be used in many situations around the garden other than in lawns. It is very tough, withstands all sorts of weather and provides an evergreen foil to other plants all year round.

Mounds

Simple grass mounds of irregular shapes made by seeding or turfing over a mound of soil adds an unusual feature to a flat garden and adds a new dimension to imaginative play for children in the garden.

For something a little more formal but still intriguing, the grass mounds can be made circular with a flat top, domed, or a taller, pyramidal shape to add extra height to the garden as a whole.

These grass structures will need to be trimmed with hand shears or a strimmer to maintain the grass.

Grass seats

These can be as simple as a low mound of grass approximately 40cm (16in) tall at the edge of a lawn or around a border that is maintained by regular strimming. This type of seat works very well where there is a change of level in the garden.

A more ambitious seat can be made from creating an area with wattle fencing or timber boarding, filling it with soil and then turfing over. This creates a very natural sitting area in the garden, although it can only be used when the weather is dry.

Patterns using different grass species

By sowing two different types of grass, each with a different shade of green, you can create a permanent pattern in the lawn. To get the different grass species, you will need to contact a grass seed supplier as normally only mixtures of seed are available from garden centres or retail outlets, rather than single species.

Prepare the area of ground in the normal way and mark out the pattern on the soil. The two types of grass seed are then sown very carefully, making sure that they do not overlap; the simpler the pattern, the easier it is to create. Maintenance of this type of feature is the same as that for any other lawn.

This elaborate grass sofa makes an unusual feature for a large garden

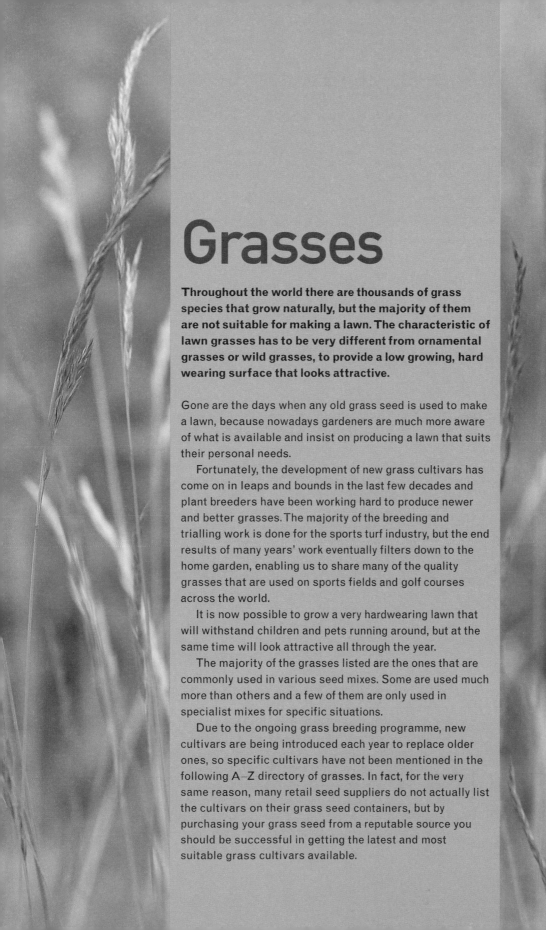

Grasses

Throughout the world there are thousands of grass species that grow naturally, but the majority of them are not suitable for making a lawn. The characteristic of lawn grasses has to be very different from ornamental grasses or wild grasses, to provide a low growing, hard wearing surface that looks attractive.

Gone are the days when any old grass seed is used to make a lawn, because nowadays gardeners are much more aware of what is available and insist on producing a lawn that suits their personal needs.

Fortunately, the development of new grass cultivars has come on in leaps and bounds in the last few decades and plant breeders have been working hard to produce newer and better grasses. The majority of the breeding and trialling work is done for the sports turf industry, but the end results of many years' work eventually filters down to the home garden, enabling us to share many of the quality grasses that are used on sports fields and golf courses across the world.

It is now possible to grow a very hardwearing lawn that will withstand children and pets running around, but at the same time will look attractive all through the year.

The majority of the grasses listed are the ones that are commonly used in various seed mixes. Some are used much more than others and a few of them are only used in specialist mixes for specific situations.

Due to the ongoing grass breeding programme, new cultivars are being introduced each year to replace older ones, so specific cultivars have not been mentioned in the following A–Z directory of grasses. In fact, for the very same reason, many retail seed suppliers do not actually list the cultivars on their grass seed containers, but by purchasing your grass seed from a reputable source you should be successful in getting the latest and most suitable grass cultivars available.

Agrostis canina (Velvet bentgrass)

Velvet bentgrass is a fine-leaved grass that spreads
by slender stolons to form a compact mat of dense
shoots. It is often used in seed mixes, because it
produces dark green leaves all year round and is
capable of growing in soils where the pH is low.
Fertilizer requirements are medium and it will
establish in both semi-shade and full sun, but it is
not very tolerant of dry soils and prefers damper
conditions in order to grow well.

Velvet bentgrass is used in seed mixes for golf
courses, bowling greens and in a garden situation
on fine quality lawns where it can be mown down
to 5mm (¼in).

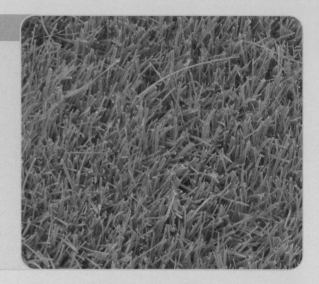

Agrostis capillaris (Browntop bent)

Browntop bent, also known as *Agrostis tenuis*, is a perennial grass
used widely in many lawn seed mixtures. Due to its ability to
establish in most soil types it is very often included in mixtures
where growing conditions are harsh, such as shady areas or dry
soils where other types of grass may find it difficult to thrive. It is
also tolerant of varying soil acidity, ranging from pH 3.0 to pH 7.0.

Browntop bent is classed as a fine grass, with narrow, hairless
pointed leaves. It produces a tufted habit and spreads by short
stolons or rhizomes. Due to its spreading habit it provides a good,
solid base to a lawn and despite its fine leaves is reasonably
hardwearing and is able to recover quickly after being trampled. It
can be mown down to 5mm (¼in) and it keeps a good green colour
through the winter months, which helps to make the lawn look
healthier and more attractive.

Due to its popularity new cultivars are continually being
introduced. As well as being bred for habit and colour, many
Browntop bents have some disease resistance to Red Thread.

Agrostis castellana (Highland bent)

Highland bent, which is sometimes called Oregon bent, is not often written about but
it is very popular in many sports turf and amenity mixtures. It is now being used more
and more in garden mixtures. The leaves are reasonably fine and a good colour,
especially during the winter months when many other grasses take on a pale
appearance. The plants spread by rhizomes to form a thick sward which can be mown
as close as 5mm (¼in). Disease, drought tolerance and wear resistance are average,
but when used as part of a mixture, Highland bent works very well and helps to keep
the lawn looking good all year round.

Agrostis stolonifera (Creeping bent)

A creeping plant with a high density of narrow leaves that spread by stolons which develop roots at their nodes where they touch damp soil. Although creeping bent has a fine leaf, the plants can become invasive and dominate a lawn unless you scarify and groom the lawn to control the creeping stems, although many of the newer cultivars are less vigorous. Creeping bent is not as widely used nowadays as it once was, although it is still a good species to use wherever you want to thicken up a sward or on banks where other grasses are slow to establish. It will grow in most soil situations but does need plenty of moisture and in dry weather soon suffers from drought. Wear tolerance is only average, but it does recover very quickly due to its strong growth. The leaves are mid-green all year round and this grass can withstand regular close mowing down to 5mm (¼in).

Cynosurus cristatus (Crested dog's tail)

This grass is not used in many lawn seed mixtures, but it is often included in wildflower and meadow mixtures. It tolerates a high pH, making it very useful in areas where the soil is chalky. Crested dog's tail has dark green narrow leaves that taper to a point. The leaves are dull on the upper surface and glossy below. It has a dense tufted habit and does not produce any rhizomes or stolons, which means it will not spread and dominate the lawn. The leaves are not as fine as a fescue or bent, but it can still be used on a fine quality lawn and will not look out of place. Unfortunately, it is slow to establish in a lawn, but when it does it is a very hard wearing grass that also recovers quickly by producing new shoots from ground level. It is also drought tolerant and can be mown down to 15mm (⅜in), but needs good light to grow well.

Festuca arundinacea (Tall fescue)

Old cultivars of this grass had coarse leaves whereas newer cultivars are much finer, making them more suitable for use as a lawn grass. The leaves are deep green and the grass is mainly tufted, although it also produces some rhizomes. The main reason new cultivars are being introduced is because tall fescue will withstand heavy wear once it is established and it is very drought tolerant. Even when under stress, this grass remains green when others have started to turn brown. It will also grow in partial shade and stand periods of water logging without being damaged, making it a very versatile grass and one that will be used more and more in grass areas that are not mown lower than 25mm (1in).

Festuca rubra commutata (Chewings fescue)

Chewings fescue is a very fine-leaved grass that is always used in a fine lawn mixture. It is a tufted grass and does not spread by stolons or rhizomes. Because of this, it can easily be swamped by more vigorous grasses. However, it does establish fairly quickly, which enables it to get a good foothold in the lawn. The leaves of Chewings fescue are tightly rolled, quite stiff and dark green in colour. It is often mixed with browntop bent or one of the other bents as they complement each other in appearance and growth. The fescue provides the top grass and the bent the bottom grass, to give a dense sward.

Because of its use on golf courses and bowling greens, many new cultivars are available and many of these are used in lawn mixtures for their good colour and compact growth. Chewings fescue can be mown down to 5mm (¼in), although it is usually allowed to grow a little longer in a lawn situation. The tips of the leaves can become yellow when cut close following a period of lush growth.

It grows best in light to medium well-drained soils, acid or alkaline. It is also added to mixtures used in dry soils and shaded areas as it is tolerant of drought conditions.

Festuca rubra rubra (Creeping red fescue)

This is another popular grass that is included in many types of seed mixture and is often listed as 'strong creeping red fescue' in catalogues and on seed containers.

The fine, tightly rolled-in leaves give the grass a bristly appearance. It is fairly strong-growing and spreads by long rhizomes which make it ideal for binding other grasses together to form a dense sward. Drought resistance is also very good and for this reason it is often used on sandy soils that dry out quickly. It also grows well in shade, so is often included in shade mixtures. The leaves vary in colour from cultivar to cultivar, but are mainly mid-green and it can be mown closely down to 5mm (¼in). Wear resistance is average, but when mixed with other grasses it produces a good sward.

Festuca rubra litoralis (Slender creeping red fescue)

Slender creeping red fescue is very similar to creeping red fescue, but as its name suggests, it has slender leaves and rhizomes. It is used in very fine grass mixtures, such as for bowling greens and golf greens, but also in general amenity and lawn mixtures. It is medium to dark green with good winter colour. It spreads by short rhizomes that produce tufted growths as they root. It wears well and because of the way it grows it recovers quickly after wear. The low growing habit and very fine leaves make it suitable for close mowing down to 5mm (¼in). It is also good in dry soils where nutrient levels are low and it can tolerate some shade.

Festuca longifolia (Hard fescue)

This grass also produces a fine sward when used as part of a mixture. The bristle-like leaves are a blue-green in colour and very narrow. It can be slow to establish, but once it is established it produces a dense tufted habit. It is ideal for areas where the soil is free draining and nutrient levels are low and it will also grow in shade, but it does not grow well in wet soils. Hard fescue can be used in both well maintained areas of grass that are mown down to 10mm (½in) or low maintenance areas where the grass is allowed to grow longer. Its main uses are on golf courses on the surrounds, lawns and shaded areas.

Festuca ovina (Sheep's fescue)

Sheep's fescue is another fine-leaved tufted grass, and like hard fescue which is similar in appearance, Sheep's fescue can also be slow to establish after sowing. It will grow in some shade and has moderate wearing abilities in a lawn situation. It is, however, drought resistant and is often used in low maintenance or meadow mixtures, but not very much in lawn mixtures. The leaves are a blue-green colour, and although it has fine leaves, it grows best when not mown too short – 20mm (¾in) is ideal for this fescue.

Lolium perenne (Perennial ryegrass)

This grass is the main ingredient for lawns that need to be hardwearing while looking good at the same time. It prefers a damp, loamy soil, although many new cultivars have been developed over recent years that will grow in most soil conditions. The original types of perennial ryegrass were strong growing and too vigorous for the average lawn, but new cultivars have been bred to be much dwarfer, making them suitable for garden use. However, some of the vigorous agricultural types of ryegrass sometimes find their way into lawn seed mixtures, so always buy quality lawn seed from a reputable source.

This grass establishes quickly from seed and produces smooth dark green shiny leaves with a distinctive red base. The new cultivars are much finer than the older agricultural types and nowadays are used on golf fairways, cricket fields and tennis courts.

Phleum bertolonii (Small-leaved Timothy)

Large-leaved Timothy is rarely used nowadays in grass mixtures due to its coarse leaves and vigorous growth, but small-leaved Timothy is used occasionally in certain mixtures. It is a reasonably hard wearing grass with a tufted habit. The leaves are broad at the base and taper to a point, but the overall appearance is a reasonably fine grass. The colour is pale green throughout the year. To grow well it needs good light, as in shady conditions it will struggle and grow very weakly. Drought resistance is average and it will grow quite happily in heavy soils. Small-leaved Timothy can be mown down to approximately 15mm (¾in).

Poa nemoralis (Wood meadow grass)

Not commonly grown in lawns, but it does have its place in some situations, as it will grow in areas where other grasses fail to thrive. Wood meadow grass is quite a tall growing grass and not suitable for a closely mown fine textured lawn, but in a meadow area, wild life garden or under trees it will be fine. It has a soft leaf that is mid-green in colour and should not be mown closer than 50mm (2in) as close regular mowing will kill it off. It will not stand heavy wear and is not good in very dry soils or periods of drought, but it will grow happily in damp and shady areas.

Poa pratensis (Smooth-stalked meadow grass)

This is a hard wearing grass that spreads across the soil by thin rhizomes. It is also known as blue grass because of the blue-green foliage. This is quite an easy grass to recognize because it produces blades of grass with parallel sides and a blunt tip, whereas most grasses have a pointed tip. When sown as a lawn mixture, it can be slow to grow and take up to twelve months to establish itself fully within a lawn, but eventually as the rhizomes are produced and the grass spreads a dense sward is formed. It is a tough, hard wearing grass and is often used with a ryegrass or on its own to give strength to a lawn. It is often used in seed mixtures required for dry sites as smooth stalked meadow grass performs and recovers well in drought conditions. It is also used in mixtures for steep banks, as the short rhizomes form a matt across the soil and help to prevent erosion. It does, however, need good light and is not suitable for growing in areas of shade. New cultivars are bred for good coloured foliage all year round, resistance to wear and dense leaf cover. Older cultivars of *Poa pratensis* disliked close mowing, although modern types used in lawn mixtures are much better and can be safely mown down to 10–15mm (½–¾in).

Poa trivialis (Rough-stalked meadow grass)

Rough-stalked meadow grass is faster to establish than smooth-stalked meadow grass and will spread quickly by stolons. The foliage is dark green with parallel sides that taper to a sharp point. Although not widely used, it is a useful grass to grow in problem areas. It does not like very light soils that dry out quickly and prefers a heavy, damp soil that is high in nutrients. In dry conditions or light sandy soils the leaves take on a reddish appearance. It will also grow in shade under trees or by the side of tall buildings, again where the soil is often damp and where other grasses may struggle to establish. Rough stalked meadow grass has average wear resistance and grows best when not mown lower than 25mm (1in). When used as part of a mixture it makes a fine utility lawn that looks good all year round. Surprisingly, despite its name, it is not at all coarse in texture.

Weed Grasses

Although lawns are made chiefly from a mixture of grass species, some grasses are classed as weed grasses. These are usually very coarse in texture, often a completely different colour, which makes them stand out from the rest of the lawn, and many types have vigorous growth.

In hard wearing lawns a few weed grasses may not cause a problem, but in a fine lawn they do spoil the appearance and should be controlled.

Eradicating them can be difficult, as they are not affected by lawn weed killers which means the only way to get rid of them is by physically digging them out or by cultural means. As most of the grasses are strong growing, some can be killed by regular close mowing or grooming prior to mowing. This continuous short cropping eventually weakens and kills them.

Maintaining a thick healthy sward will also help to prevent the weed grasses getting a foot hold, as will sweeping away worm casts that act as a seed bed for broad-leaved and grass weeds to grow in.

Agropyron repens (Couch grass)

Agropyron is also known as *Elymus repens* and has many local names such as couch, twitch, quack grass, Scotch quelch and dog grass. It is a vigorous creeping perennial with dark green leaves. It spreads rapidly by cream-coloured underground rhizomes that are very brittle and when dug out of the soil will break into several pieces. From each section of the root a new plant quickly develops. It also grows from seed in the soil, so even removing all the roots is not a guarantee of getting rid of it. In lawns it tends to be a problem only in newly sown lawns where it competes with young grasses. Fortunately, it does not stand being mown closely and where it does grow in a newly seeded lawn a season of regular mowing will normally kill it off.

Dactylis glomerata (Cock's foot)

Cocks foot or orchard grass as it is also known is a strong growing perennial that forms a large clump of grass that is very tough and woody at the base. The leaves are blue-green in colour and have a rough texture. In a pasture it will grow to approximately 60cm (2ft) or more and produce a large seed head which gives it the name of cock's foot.

In a lawn situation it is a troublesome weed that produces areas of coarse grass, often with a dry centre of dead plant material. Very close mowing will kill it eventually, but on an average lawn that is maintained to around 15–20mm (½–¾in) it will survive. Raking the areas with a wire rake before mowing will have some effect by lifting the leaves, but by far the best method of control is to cut out the clump and either re-seed or re-turf the patch.

It is also important to maintain the lawn and keep a thick grass covering to prevent seeds germinating in worn patches or areas where the grass cover is thin.

Holcus lanata (Yorkshire fog)

Yorkshire fog is a hairy perennial that is also called velvet grass and meadow soft grass. The greyish-green leaves are covered in soft hairs and the base of the stem is white with pink stripes, which make it very easy to identify. It grows and establishes very easily from seed and will thrive in damp soil conditions.

In fine lawns Yorkshire fog can be a nuisance, as the pale coloured broad leaf-blades grow very fast and stand above the dark green fine grasses to make the lawn look pale and patchy. Grooming followed by close mowing will gradually weaken the grass, as will slashing the clumps with a knife before mowing.

In roughly mown areas it does not cause a problem and will give a good grass cover, especially in wet soils where many cultivated grasses are difficult to establish.

Holcus mollis (Creeping soft grass)

This is very similar in appearance to Yorkshire fog, but the leaves are less hairy. The main difference is that it produces tough rhizomes that when cut re-grow into new plants. This makes it very difficult to control in a lawn situation and even when mown very closely it will re-grow from the rhizomes below the soil.

Fortunately, in lawns it is not as common as Yorkshire fog as it prefers to grow in shady woodland areas, but where it does start to colonize a lawn the best method of control is to spray the creeping soft grass out with a translocated weed killer which will kill the rhizomes, and then re-seed or turf the patch in.

Poa annua (Annual meadow grass)

Annual meadow grass, also called annual bluegrass, is a low growing grass that grows in clumps. It is tolerated in many lawns and actually forms a large percentage of the summer grass cover. It grows and establishes very quickly from seed, producing a mid-green coloured plant. The flower heads are produced on very short stems that are often below the height of cut, which means it seeds freely in the lawn. Annual meadow grass rapidly colonizes bare patches of earth and during a summer there will be several generations of the plant. The main disadvantage is that annual meadow grass is susceptible to drought and as soon as the soil starts to dry out the grass turns yellow and dies, making the lawn look very patchy. Control is difficult, but grooming to lift the flower spikes prior to mowing will reduce the production of seed. If the lawn is thin, over-sowing in the autumn will help to thicken the sward.

Mosses, Lichens & Algae

Mosses, lichen and algae are all primitive non-flowering plants that have adapted to grow in lawns. Although they do not kill the grass, they can make it look unsightly and will make mowing and other maintenance difficult.

There are many hundreds of different species of moss that grow in the wild, but most of them do not grow in a lawn situation. Many of these mosses, including the ones that do colonize in lawns, are very attractive when you study them closely and have intricate leaves in spirals or flat rows and unusual fruiting bodies.

All types of moss produce spores, not seeds, and have a very simple plant structure. They do not have a proper root system like most other plants; instead, they produce a modified stem with root-like structures called rhizoids that anchor them to the ground. They are also able to reproduce by small fragments of the plant that break off; hence the reason moss should always be killed before being raked out of the lawn.

Mosses vary greatly, but most species produce male and female parts closely together on the same plant. In order for fertilization and the production of spores and fruiting capsules to develop, moist conditions must be present. Many mosses are also capable of withstanding very dry weather during the summer months when they enter their dormant period.

Lichens and algae are also very simple plant structures and can be a problem in the lawn. Consequently, they should be dealt with as soon as possible.

Mosses, lichens and algae are not affected by lawn weed killers, but sulphate of iron does keep them under control. However, the fact that they are there in the first place is an indication that there is an underlying problem such as compaction, shade, surface drainage or poor soil, and these should also be corrected.

Fern-like or trailing moss

These mosses are present in many lawns and have very soft, feathery stems that are usually light green in colour, although different species vary. They are usually found in damp areas that are in semi-shade or where drainage is slow or on neglected lawns. When present in large amounts the lawn will be very soft and spongy to walk on, due to the open growth of the plant. The two main types of this fern-like moss are Hyphum and Eurhynchium and they produce fruiting capsules that contain spores in autumn and winter, although some species only produce small amounts. Some species will establish in a wide range of soils, whereas others need either acid or alkaline conditions to get a foot hold, but they all need moisture. Treatment to control them should be undertaken in early spring or autumn.

Mat-forming moss

This type of moss can be very troublesome, especially on acid soils. The small upright stems grow to around 1–2.5cm (½–1in) and are grouped very closely together to form mats of moss. The two common types usually found in lawns are Bryum and Ceratodon, and unless the patches are checked or controlled they can become quite large. Bryum is the more compact of the two and is very dense in habit; it will smother fine grasses in some situations. Small drooping capsules that are often pear-shaped are produced in spring where the lawn has not been closely mown.

  The other common mat-forming moss is *Ceratodon purpureus* and this is often referred to as 'winter moss' because it seems to die out in the spring when the grass starts to grow and then reappear in the autumn. This moss grows slightly taller and can be recognized by the leaves, which are often tinged reddish-brown. The fruit capsules are also produced in spring.

Upright moss

These mosses are mainly found in lawns that that have dry areas, especially where the soil is acid. They are not generally as troublesome as other types of moss.

  Their habit is upright and the plants produce dark green tufts of stems that can grow to 10cm (4in) or more depending on the species. However, the same plants can adapt to conditions where the grass is mown regularly by only growing to 2.5cm (1in). In areas that are not kept short the capsules will develop during the summer. These are four sided in shape and very often the male plant will produce pinkish rosettes of leaves at the same time.

Dog lichen

Lichens can be very attractive to look at and there are many types that grow in damp crevices and on trees to form clusters of ferny growths. These are generally a sign of clean, pure air.

This is an unusual plant which is a combination of a fungus and algae. The process is complex and not fully understood although it is known that they both obtain food by different methods and feed one another in a symbiotic relationship.

The one that normally grows in lawns is dog lichen, *Peltigera canina*, which grows where conditions are damp, where there is a build up of thatch or under the shade of trees. The leaf-like structures can be 3–4cm (1½in) across and are almost black on top when wet; they curl at the edges to reveal a cream coloured underside. When the weather is dry, the upper surface of the lichen changes to a much paler colour. Whitish root-like structures are also produced underneath. Dog lichen looks like fallen leaves that have worked their way into the sward.

Control is by using a moss killer that contains sulphate of iron, but as is the case with moss, the growing conditions of the lawn should also be improved to prevent them from returning.

Green algae

Algae are very simple green plants without roots, stems, leaves or flowers. Most algae live in water and create a green haze, but some types are able to live on damp soil.

On a lawn they tend to be a problem where there are bare patches or soil or on a new lawn where the sward is very thin. Unlike moss, algae prefer good sun light to develop and they will establish to form a dark green slimy scum over the soil surface that turns black as it dries out. This capping over the soil not only looks unsightly, it also prevents air and water penetrating into the ground. Scarifying and aerating the lawn will help to get rid of it, as will applying moss killer or lawn sand. Feeding to thicken up the sward will also make it very difficult for the algae to grow.

Algal slime

This is caused by several types of algae that produce a dark green or black jelly-like slime on the surface of the lawn that is also known as 'squidge'. Apart from looking messy on the lawn, the slime is very slippery and can be dangerous to walk on or operate machinery on. It tends to develop on bare patches or areas of thin grass where the soil is compact as a result of heavy wear. It can also occur in shady conditions, where drainage is poor and where the nutrient levels are low. Where it appears it should be physically removed with a brush or the back of a rake. Applying sulphate of iron or lawn sand will help to prevent it growing again, possibly because this has an acidifying effect on the soil. Improving the lawn by aeration, scarifying and top-dressing with a sandy mixture will also help.

Broad-Leaved Weeds

Weeds will always find their way into a lawn, especially a new one that has been seeded. Even in established lawns that are well maintained, there is no escaping broad-leaved weeds.

Most weeds will grow from seed that is carried in on people's shoes or by birds and mammals, and they only need a very small amount of growing space between the blades of grass in order to germinate and establish. Others may creep into the lawn from the surrounding garden. Some weeds are easy to get rid of, while others are very difficult to eliminate completely from the lawn.

The way to treat weeds growing in your lawn is up to you and the type of lawn you are trying to create. Some gardeners will not tolerate any weeds at all growing in their lush green sward and will treat their lawn annually with a selective weedkiller or get down on their hands and knees to remove the weeds by hand. Other gardeners are quite happy for a few of the smaller-leaved weeds to grow in the lawn and will only control large invasive weeds.

Weeds can be controlled by various methods such as hand weeding, scarifying and lawn grooming prior to mowing and the use of a selective lawn weedkiller that kills broad-leaved plants but not grass. Keeping the grass thick and healthy will also make it much more difficult for weeds to establish in the lawn.

If you wish to create a natural or wild life area in your garden, many of the so-called lawn weeds can actually be grown as wildflowers, or you may consider allowing some weeds to flower in spring to add interest to the lawn.

On the following pages the most common broad-leaved lawn weeds are listed, along with a selection of other plants that can be included in a wildflower lawn.

Achillea millefolium (Yarrow)

Yarrow is a perennial weed that has very fine fern-like leaves. It spreads by creeping underground stems to produce a strong growing plant and in some situations can be a very invasive weed. It produces white or pinkish flowers during the summer, although in lawns mown regularly these are not able to develop. It will grow in most soil types but prefers a sandy, well-drained soil and it is able to withstand drought conditions. Control of yarrow is difficult, due to the fineness of its foliage. Selective lawn weed killers have little effect once the weed is established. Hand weeding will have some effect, but it will re-establish very quickly from just a few shoots left in the ground. Grooming the lawn prior to mowing will lift the long stems so that they can be cut off. Feeding the lawn on a regular basis to improve the thickness of the sward will help to suppress it.

Aphanes arvensis (Parsley piert)

This is a close growing weed with short stalks and fan-shaped leaves with hairy stems. Although not as common as many other lawn weeds, it can be a problem in areas where the soil is light and sandy. It also thrives on acid soils. It is an annual and can produce several generations in one season. The small green flowers are produced very close to the ground, meaning it can easily produce seed even on regularly mown lawns. Parsley piert is more of a problem on lawns that are mown very closely and for this reason it is a good idea to lift the height of cut slightly to allow the grass to grow a little longer. Feeding the lawn will also help as, like several other weeds, it prefers soils low in nutrients. Lawn weedkiller will also control the weed, especially when applied as a spray.

Bellis perennis (Daisy)

This is perhaps one of the most recognizable of all lawn weeds because of its white- or pink-coloured flowers that are produced in spring and early summer. A cultivated form is also used as a spring bedding plant and various forms are available with pink, red or white large double flowers. The Bellis that we consider to be a weed is a very adaptable plant and will grow in most types of soil, whether it is wet or dry, acid and alkaline, although it grows particularly well in moist, loamy soils. It is a perennial weed that produces a rosette of spoon-shaped glossy leaves. Once established, it produces a mass of ground hugging stems and will smother areas of fine grass.

Mowing as a method of control has little or no effect as daisies will grow quite happily in both very short and long grass. The easiest method of control is to use lawn sand, a granular feed and weed or a selective lawn weedkiller spray. Hand weeding is also an effective method of control. If you wish to create flower circles within your lawn, daisies are one of the best wildflowers to use (see Other Lawn Features, page 98).

Centaurea nigra (Lesser knapweed or hardheads)

Knapweed is a perennial of grassland and road verges, but not a major lawn weed, as close regular mowing will keep it under control or even kill it. It is, however, a good plant to grow in natural or wildflower areas, where it grows to approximately 45cm (18in) tall. The deep pink brush-like flowers are produced on tall stems during the summer. It will grow in most soils, including chalky and damp soils where it will soon establish and naturalize. To prevent the main plant being killed by mowing, avoid cutting lower than 50mm (2in).

Centaurea cyanus (Cornflower)

This is a well-known annual wildflower that is often associated with other cornfield annuals such as poppies and corn marigold. It is not a lawn weed and even if allowed to seed in the garden it would not establish in an established sward.

Once a common site in the countryside, cornflower is now rarely seen as a result of modern farming practices. However, it can be easily grown in a garden on an area of bare soil or in the lawn where a piece of turf has been removed to expose the soil. Seed can be sown in autumn or spring into the cultivated soil. Cornflowers are not particularly fussy and will grow in most well-drained soils. They grow to around 60–75cm (24–30in) with grey-green downy foliage and bright blue flowers through the summer and should self-seed.

Cerastium holosteoides (Mouse ear)

This is a small-leaved perennial weed that produces a mat of closely growing hairy stems with small white flowers. It is a ubiquitous lawn weed and grows in most soils, favouring poor soils that are low in nutrients, but it does not tolerate acid soils with a low pH. The stems and leaves grow close to the soil and root at intervals as they spread. Small flowers are produced from late spring through the summer until early autumn. As well as creeping through the sward, it also seeds into small bare patches or worm casts and if left unchecked will soon form large areas.

Fortunately, this weed is reasonably easy to control in a lawn situation. Small isolated plants can be removed by hand or where there are patches of the weed, a selective lawn weedkiller can be applied either as a weed and feed or spray.

Chrysanthemum segetum (Corn marigold)

This is another cornfield annual that can easily be grown from seed into an area of cultivated ground. It is a member of the daisy family and produces attractive golden-yellow daisy-like flowers during the summer. The foliage is bright green and the plants grow to approximately 45cm (18in). Although an annual, in a mild winter the plants may survive and grow and flower for a second time, but for the best flowers and strongest plants, fresh seed should be sown annually, or the old flowers allowed to self-seed. To grow well, it prefers a well-drained lightly cultivated soil. Like other tall growing annuals, corn marigold is never a problem in lawns.

Cirsium spp. (Thistle)

There are several different types of thistle that grow in gardens, but most of them are not a serious lawn weed as close mowing usually kills them off. The creeping thistle *Cirsium arvense* can be a problem in newly sown lawns. This is a perennial plant with prickly leaves that are woolly when young, turning blue-green in colour when older. It spreads quickly by producing creeping roots. The lilac-coloured flowers are produced in summer and the whole plant dies down in the autumn back to the underground roots. Regular, fairly close mowing will usually kill creeping thistles. *C. acaule* or the stemless thistle produces a rosette of leaves that grow very close to the ground, and this can usually survive in lawns that are mown longer that 2.5cm (1in). The long leaves are very prickly and hairy on the underside. The mauve-coloured flower is produced from the centre of the rosette.

Where there are only a few thistles in the lawn, they can be cut out by hand, although they may re-grow from the root. Both granular and liquid lawn weedkillers are very effective at controlling them.

Crepis capillaris (Smooth hawksbeard)

This is an annual that sometimes grows as a short-lived perennial plant that is very common on road verges and rough grassland such as orchards or wildflower meadows. It produces shiny leaves and flower spikes with loose clusters of yellow flowers throughout the summer. The flowers are quite small and the whole plant only grows to around 45–60cm (18–24in) tall. In a well maintained lawn hawksbeard is not normally a problem, as regular close mowing will prevent it from establishing. In longer grass where it becomes a problem, it can be controlled easily by using a selective lawn weedkiller or by hand pulling before the flower self seeds.

Galium saxatile (Heath bedstraw)

Although not a serious lawn weed, heath bedstraw will grow in lawns because of its low growing, almost prostrate habit. It is a perennial that produces hairless stems and sharply pointed leaves that grow along the ground to form a mat. The flowers are white and produced in small clusters along the stems from early summer onwards.

It prefers acid, well-drained conditions and is often found in infertile soils. In mown lawns it grows close to the soil, but if allowed to grow would reach approximately 20cm (8in).

Lawn weedkillers will control it, although it may be necessary to make more than one application. Due to the small foliage, sprays are more effective than a granular weedkiller.

Galium vernum (Lady's bedstraw)

Lady's bedstraw is a perennial plant and very common on road verges and in well-drained soils. It is said to get its name from the legend that Mary gave birth to Jesus on a bed stuffed with the plant. It is not a serious weed of closely mown lawns, but it will establish in lawns that are allowed to grow a little longer where the sprawling stems can grow outwards. It is also a good plant to grow in a small meadow area, where it will produce its bright yellow flowers in clusters along the wiry stems that are covered in whorls of tiny dark green leaves. These flowers are produced from early summer through to early autumn. It is not a plant that you would normally want to control, although selective lawn weedkiller will kill it when applied through a sprayer.

Geranium spp. (Cranesbill)

The geranium family is quite large and there are many annual and biennial species that will grow in newly sown lawns or rough mown areas where the grass is not very thick. Dove's foot cranesbill, *Geranium molle*, has pale pink flowers and small-flowered cranesbill, *G. pussilum*, has delicate lilac flowers that are produced during the summer. Both of the annual types are very common and make a semi-spreading plant that grows to around 30cm (12in) if not mown. They will, however, grow in rough grass that is mown down to approximately 7.5cm (3in) as they will grow and spread sideways.

Another annual/biennial geranium is herb Robert, *Geranium robertianum* (pictured), which is taller growing than most varieties and will reach approximately 45cm (18in). It grows in woodland or semi-shade and can be sown as a wildflower where in natural areas the grass cover is thin.

Geranuim pratensis (Meadow cranesbill)

This is a perennial geranium of grassland and can be found growing in meadows and on road verges. In a lawn situation it will not survive, as close, regular mowing will kill it. It is, however, an excellent wildflower to grow if you want to create a meadow area. The plants are herbaceous and die down in the winter and regrow in a clump the following spring. Their ultimate height can be up to 60cm (24in), but this varies depending on location and soil type and in many cases they do not grow as tall. The large blue flowers are produced mainly in early summer, but they often produce small flushes of flower through the summer until early autumn.

Hypochaeris radicata (Cat's ear)

Cat's ear is a perennial weed that can be a problem on some lawns and will grow in most soil types. The hairy toothed leaves grow in a rosette close to the ground, so although regular mowing will cut off the flower spike, the main plant will survive below the height of cut. The yellow dandelion-like flowers are produced on tall wiry stems usually two at a time, from late spring through to early autumn.

In a wildflower area, such as a meadow or a specific area in the garden, the plant looks very well suited, but in a lawn the rosettes spoil the appearance of the sward and should be removed. Hand weeding can be done, but the entire tap root needs to be removed to prevent weed growth. The best method of control is to use a selective weedkiller as a spray or in granular form. New plants also grow very easily from seed in small bare patches on the lawn.

Knautia arvensis (Field scabious)

Field scabious is a lovely perennial meadow plant that is often seen growing in hedgerows and road verges. It grows to 60–75cm (24–30in), depending on the soil type and growing conditions. The very attractive bluish-lilac flowers grow on tall stems and have a flattish head from early summer into the autumn if the plants are allowed to grow freely. In a lawn field scabious is not a weed, as it will not grow in closely mown conditions, but it is ideal for using in a meadow area where it will grow happily. When flowering is finished the area can be mown down to 5cm (2in) without damaging the main plant, which will lie dormant over winter and start into growth again the following spring. The best way to introduce the plant into a meadow is as small plants in spring or autumn.

Leontodon hispidus (Rough hawkbit)

This is a perennial weed which has a deep fleshy tap root and will grow in most soil types. The leaves are like a dandelion, long and shallowly lobed, but covered with very short bristly hairs that give the leaf a rough texture. The yellow flowers are borne singularly on tall stiff stems and occasionally the outer florets are tinged with red or orange. Rough hawkbit will grow as a lawn weed, especially where the grass is now closely mown. It is also used in natural areas where the foliage will grow more upright. The total height of the plant is around 45cm (18in). Individual roots can be dug out, but unless the root is removed it will produce new shoots from below ground level. Selective weedkiller applied in late spring usually works very well due to the large leaf area.

Leucanthemum vulgare (Ox-eye daisy)

Ox-eye daisy, also called dog daisy, is a familiar site on many motorway verges in early summer, with its large, white daisy flowers. It is a perennial that grows in grass land and will quickly spread to form large areas of plants. It grows in most soils, clay or sand and spreads by the original plant multiplying each year and through self seeding. Young plants can be introduced to a meadow area or seed can be sown in small areas of bare soil. When established it grows to approximately 60cm (2ft).

It can become a weed in mown lawns and will form a low growing clump of plants where the grass is mown to no lower than 25mm (1in), but in this situation it will not flower. An application of a lawn weed killer will kill plants in a lawn if they become invasive. When grown in a meadow, the plants should be cut down in late summer.

Lotus corniculatus (Bird's-foot trefoil)

This is a perennial plant that is also called bacon and eggs because of its coloured flowers. Bird's-foot trefoil is very widespread and grows in grass land, road verges and is also a weed in lawns. In long grass it will grow up to 30cm (12in), but in a mown lawn it takes on a prostrate habit and grows very close to the ground. It is a member of the pea family and has leaves with five leaflets, but the back two are attached to the stem and fold backwards to give the appearance of three leaflets – hence trefoil. The pea-shaped flowers are yellow and often tinged orange or red, but the colour does vary from region to region. These are produced over several months through the summer and are followed by long thin seed pods. To control the weed in lawns, hand weeding can be done to remove small amounts and grooming before mowing will stand the long stems upright so that they can be cut off. Selective weedkillers can be used, but more than one application may be needed over the season.

Luzula campestris (Field woodrush)

Field woodrush is often mistaken for grass in a lawn situation, but it has broader, thicker leaves that are covered in white hairs. It also produces short flower spikes with brown flowers. It is often found on drier, acid soils, although it will grow in most soils, including clay. Control is difficult as most lawn weedkillers have little or no effect on the plant and several applications are needed to have any effect at all. Liming the soil will make conditions less favourable for field woodrush, but this can lead to other problems, such as altering the existing grass population. The best method of dealing with it is to feed the grass and encourage a thick sward.

Medicago lupulina (Black medick)

This annual weed can be a serious problem in fine lawns as it grows flat to the ground and is difficult to control with weed killer. It is a small weed that has a clover-like leaf and is often mixed up with yellow suckling clover, *Trifolium dubium*. The plants produce slender horizontal branches from the base of the plant. The leaves are made up of three leaflets that sometimes have a very small point on the end. The small yellow flowers are produced in summer on short stalks growing from the leaf joints. Small black seed pods are also produced on the plant which when ripe split open to distribute the seed. Hand weeding can be done by tracing the shoots back to the main root, but it is a slow job. A selective lawn weedkiller can be sprayed, but several applications may be needed as new seedlings will be growing through the summer.

Papaver rhoeas (Field poppy)

This is an annual plant of cultivated land and is not a lawn weed, as it will not grow in managed grassland. It can be grown very easily as a cornfield annual, along with yellow corn marigold and blue cornflowers to provide a colourful display during the summer months. To grow it needs an area of bare soil where the surface has been loosened by raking. The seed can be sown in autumn or spring into the flowering position. Once established it normally self-seeds and grows again the following year. It will grow in most soils that are well-drained.

Plantago lanceolata
(Ribwort plantain)

Ribwort plantain is a widespread perennial lawn weed and will grow in most garden soils, ranging from very sandy to heavy clay. *Plantago lanceolata* produces long narrow leaves that are heavily ribbed, hence its common name. These form a large rosette that can suffocate fine grasses.

During the summer, long flower spikes develop from the centre of the rosette with short brown flowers and cream stamens. New plants from seed establish very quickly in small areas of bare soil and if the plants are not controlled they will take over a lawn.

Fortunately, ribwort plantains are reasonably easy to control either by hand weeding or with a lawn weedkiller applied when the plants are growing. In a wide area the tall flower spikes can look decorative.

Plantago major
(Greater plantain)

Another common perennial lawn weed, often called broad-leaved plantain. It produces large rosettes or pale green leaves that grow very flat to the ground. Like ribwort plantain, these large leaves can spoil the appearance of a fine lawn and kill fine grasses. The flowers are greenish spikes that grow from the centre of the rosette. Greater plantain grows in most soils. Control is either by removing by hand or the use of a selective lawn weedkiller.

Plantago media
(Hoary plantain)

Hoary plantain has large leaves that look like a cross between ribwort and greater plantain – broad and long. However, unlike the other leaves which are smooth, hoary plantain leaves are covered in fine hairs that give a downy appearance and texture.

The flowers are also produced on spikes during the summer, but they are larger and the stamens have a pinkish-purple tinge and are sweetly scented.

Control of this perennial weed is by hand or selective weedkiller. When the weeds have been removed from the lawn the bare patches of soil should be patched in with seed or turf to prevent seedling plantains from establishing.

Potentilla anserina (Silverweed)

Silverweed is not a common lawn weed, but in lawns that are neglected or where the soil is damp it can be a problem. It is a perennial weed that spreads by creeping stems that root at their nodes and quickly form a dense mat of foliage. The leaves are pinnate; made up of several leaflets on one stems and often green on top and silvery below. The yellow flowers are borne along the stem from late spring until late summer.

Hand weeding to get rid of silverweed is difficult, because it roots in so many places along the long stems, making a lawn weedkiller the most efficient option. This should be applied when the weed is in full growth and it may be necessary to give a second application where the weed is heavy.

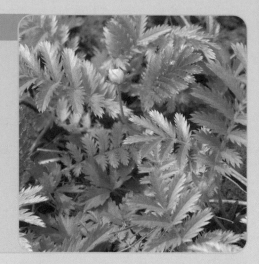

Primula veris (Cowslip)

Cowslips naturally grow in meadows and grassy places and are ideal for growing in lawns that are not mown too short, or a wildflower meadow where they will be allowed to seed. Their leaves are formed in a low growing rosette and as long as you do not mow lower than 5–7.5cm (2–3in) the plant will be fine. Clusters of the deep yellow flowers are carried on long stems in mid- to late spring and after they have finished flowering mowing can continue as normal. If you want the plants to seed naturally to get more plants in the grass, they should be left until late summer.

Two close relatives of the cowslip can also be grown in the lawn. Primroses, *Primula vulgaris*, and oxlip, *Primula elatior*, will both grow in grass and all three will often hybridize with each other.

Prunella vulgaris (Self-heal)

This is a perennial weed with a creeping habit. In long meadow grass the plants will grow to 30cm (12in) or more, but in closely mown turf it can grow and flower very close to the ground. It grows in a wide range of soils, including damp, clay soils. The stems are square and as it creeps through the lawn it roots at intervals to create a dense cover. The leaves are large, green and oval with a point. Flowerheads made up of many small flowers are produced in early summer, but flowering often continues through the summer into early autumn. These are usually purple in colour, although occasionally pink or white flowers are produced.

Self-heal makes a very good flowering plant for a meadow or natural area, but in a formal closely mown lawn it can be invasive if not controlled. Hand weeding is difficult because of the spread of the plants, but lawn weedkiller works very well.

Ranunculus bulbosus (Bulbous buttercup)

Buttercups are well-known for their yellow flowers in spring and early summer. The bulbous buttercup naturally grows in meadows and produces a swollen base, from which it gets its name. It grows in many soils but will tolerate drier conditions than other types of buttercup. In a lawn it can be a serious weed and can be difficult to control even with lawn weedkillers. The cut-leaves and flower spikes grow from the bulbous base in spring and die down in late autumn. Hand weeding is a good method of control where numbers are not too great, or spraying with a lawn weedkiller in late spring and again in the summer.

Ranunculus ficaria (Lesser celandine)

This pretty yellow spring flowering plant will soon take over a border, especially if the soil is moist. It will also grow in a shady lawn, especially where the soil is damp and the grass is not cut short. The plants grow in spring from underground bulbils and spread by short creeping stems. The leaves are a glossy green and the yellow flowers are produced from mid- to late spring. Shortly after flowering has finished the plants naturally die down and remain dormant until the following spring. Digging out the small bulbils will help, but if any of the tiny bulbils are left in the soil, the plant will still grow. Spraying with a lawn weedkiller will also help, but because the plants die down in early summer there is not time to carry out repeat sprays.

Ranunculus repens (Creeping buttercup)

Creeping buttercups grow very close to the ground and produce stolons that root at the nodes. They can spread across a lawn extremely quickly, especially in wet, heavy soils, which suit their growing conditions best. Mowing does not kill the plants and occasionally flowers will develop almost at ground level.

When allowed to grow naturally the flowers are produced on long stems in late spring to mid-summer and the plants grow to around 45–60cm (18–24in). The leaves are divided into three main leaflets and form a dense mat over the lawn. Creeping buttercups are so invasive in a lawn that they are much easier to control with lawn weedkillers than the bulbous buttercup.

Treatment should start in late spring when the plants are growing actively and have produced a good cover of leaves to absorb the weedkiller.

Rumex acetosella (Sheep's sorrel)

This is a perennial weed that can be a nuisance in lawns on sandy acid soils where it thrives. It produces underground stems and creeps across the lawn. The leaves are arrow shaped and turn out at the stalk end to create a distinctive shape. The leaves often turn red and this is an indication that the soil is acid. Hand weeding is impractical because of the creeping underground stems, but lawn weedkiller is very effective at killing sheep's sorrel, although more than one application may be needed.

Common sorrel, *Rumex acetosa*, is closely related, but is not as much of a problem weed in the lawn.

Sagina procumbens (Pearlwort)

This is a small perennial weed that looks very similar to grass in a fine, closely mown lawn. It has very narrow leaves and produces spreading stolons that grow quickly to form dense areas of the weed which will smother fine grasses. Small white flowers are also produced and it is these that often bring the weed to people's attention. It grows in most types of soils, but tends to be worse on very short lawns where the nutrient levels are low. Pearlwort is fairly easy to control with a lawn weedkiller, but once you have killed it, it is worth feeding the lawn to thicken up the grass sward and avoid mowing too closely in future.

Senecio jacobaea (Ragwort)

Ragwort is a problem weed in road verges and grassland where it seeds itself and spreads very quickly. It is easily recognized by its tall stems that branch out at the top and are covered in small golden-yellow, daisy-like flowers in the summer, followed by masses of tiny seeds that drift in the breeze. It is a biennial or short-lived perennial and will grow in most soils. In a lawn situation it will quickly establish if flowering plants are close by and produce a rosette of cut-leaves that grow close to the ground. It will not flower due to regular mowing, but the spread of the weed leaves will smother fine grasses. Control is by hand weeding which is very easy, or with a lawn weedkiller.

Ragwort is the food supply of the orange and black ringed cinnabar moth caterpillars, but it is also poisonous to horses and cattle.

Senecio vulgaris (Groundsel)

Groundsel is a low growing annual weed that grows on cultivated land and ground that has been disturbed. In new lawns from seed it can establish quickly, especially in the spring. As lawn weedkillers cannot be used on young grass, it should be controlled by hand weeding if the plants are smothering the grass. Fortunately, it is killed quickly by mowing, so by the time the new lawn has been mown two or three times the weeds will have disappeared. On established lawns, groundsel is never a problem.

Stellaria media (Chickweed)

Chickweed is another annual weed that grows on cultivated soil and can be a problem in the spring on newly sown lawns. It quickly forms large areas of soft stems that produce small white flowers. It can grow flower and seed several times in a season if left alone. In a new lawn, large clumps of the weed can be pulled by hand, but mowing is perhaps the best way of controlling it. Occasionally it will persist in the lawn for several months growing close to the ground, but as the grass establishes and thickens the chickweed will gradually be weakened and die out. In established lawns chickweed can sometimes grow in places where there is bare soil or where the grass is thin and weak. Feeding to improve the grass and regular mowing will kill it, as will an application of lawn weedkiller.

Sonchas olerceus (Sow thistle)

This is another weed that tends to grow in newly sown areas of grass. The annual sow thistle grows very quickly and produces light green leaves with soft spiny edges. The pale yellow flowers are borne in clusters and develop into seed heads. In cultivated land, annual sow thistle can grow to around 90cm (3ft) or taller. Although regular mowing will kill them off, it may be necessary to chop them off at the base or hand pull the plants to prevent them smothering the new grass.

The perennial sow thistle, *Sonchas arvensis*, which looks very similar, will sometimes grow in thinly covered grass land that is only occasionally mown. It is not a problem weed in lawns that are mown and maintained regularly.

Taraxacum officinale (Dandelion)

This weed is easily recognized by its yellow flowers and round, hairy seed heads. It prefers a heavy loam soil where it can develop a thick tap root, although it will grow in just about any soil. Thousands of seeds produced by each plant are carried by the wind and usually grow the following season on worm casts or small bare patches on the soil. In a lawn dandelions can be a problem, as the large rosettes of flat growing leaves smother and kill the grass and this allows more of the weeds to establish. Dandelions can be dug out by hand, but if a small piece of the root is left in the soil a new plant will grow. The best method of control is to use a lawn weedkiller, either as a granular feed and weed or spray. Once the weeds have been killed, over-seed the patches to create a thick sward to prevent new dandelions from establishing.

Trifolium repens (White clover)

This is a creeping perennial weed that establishes very quickly in a lawn. It will grow in most soils although it is not as troublesome in very acid conditions. Each leaf has three leaflets that have a pale marking in the centre. The creeping stems grow across the lawn and root at regular intervals from the leaf nodes. The size and vigour of clover can vary and in some lawns the leaves are very small, whereas in others they can be large and lush. White flowers sometimes tinged with pink, which tend to attract bees and other insects, are produced through the summer even on lawns that are mown regularly. Many gardeners will live with clover in their lawns as it is always a green colour, even in a dry summer, and the nitrogen fixing nodules on the roots also supply some food to the grass. If you do wish to control it, a selective lawn weedkiller applied as a spray is the most effective method, but more than one application may be needed.

Trifolium dubium (Yellow suckling clover)

This is a small annual clover that is also known as lesser trefoil. It is often mixed up with black medick, *Medicago lupulina*, as they both look similar. In a lawn it can be a serious problem, as it is able to grow in well established sward. The plant spreads out from a single stem growing out of the soil to form a mat of growth very close to the ground. The small clover-like leaves are very slightly notched, but you need to examine the leaves at close quarters to see them. Along the stems small yellow flowers are produced, but unlike black medick which has black seed pods, the flowers in yellow suckling clover fade and turn brown. Control is either by carefully weeding the plants out by hand or by using a lawn weedkiller. To get good control of the weed it is normal to spray several times during the summer months as it is a difficult weed to kill.

Veronica spp. (Speedwell)

There are several types of speedwell but the two that are most commonly found on lawns are Germander speedwell, *Veronica chamaedrys*, and slender speedwell, *Veronica filiformis*. Both are creeping perennials with oval to round toothed leaves and will form a dense mat in the lawn and will grow in most types of soil. The flowers of germander speedwell are bright blue with a white eye and slender speedwell has mauve flowers. Their main flowering period is between mid-spring to mid-summer, but a few flowers are often produced through to early autumn. Germander speedwell is sometimes used when establishing a meadow, where it can grow up to 30cm (12in). Of the two, slender speedwell is the most troublesome in a lawn. Control of all speedwells is difficult, as they are resistant to many lawn weedkillers and hand weeding is not easy. When using a lawn weedkiller, always apply it through a sprayer to coat the leaves with a fine mist, from spring onwards.

Veronica serpyllifolia (Thyme-leaved speedwell)

This speedwell is not as common as other types, but when it does get into a lawn it can be quite invasive. It is a low, creeping perennial with small, oval, smooth leaves in pairs along the stem. As it creeps through the grass it produces roots from the leaf joints and will quickly form a large dense mat of weed. The flowers are very small and pale blue or white in colour and produced in spring to early summer. In closely mown lawns the flowers are often not seen. Thyme-leaved speedwell will grow in most soils but it prefers a moist, heavy soil. Like other types of speedwell it is also quite difficult to control and needs spraying with a lawn weedkiller from early in the season. Grooming prior to mowing to lift the creeping stems will also help and always use the grass box on the lawn mower as small pieces of the plant will root easily.

Vicia spp. (Vetch)

Vetches are not a weed of mown lawns as they grow in long grass or bare soil. There are many different types of vetch and they make a welcome addition to a wildflower area or meadow. Most are clambering plants that use the taller grasses as support. They are members of the pea family and produce pea-like flowers in various shades of blue, purple and pink. Many vetches, such as the upright vetch, *Vicia orobus*, are perennial and die down in autumn, regrowing the following spring. Others such as common vetch, *Vicia sativa*, are annuals and grow from seed in spring.

Grass Alternatives

We think of a lawn as a thick carpet of lush green grass, but a lawn does not have to be made from grass and there are many other plants that are suitable. The reason grasses are used in lawns is because they are hard wearing, look attractive and above all are able to withstand regular mowing in order to keep them short and tidy. From a practical point of view, grass is the best choice for a lawn and this is reflected in the fact that grass is used on so many sports and amenity areas.

However, for decorative and ornamental purposes, a lawn can be made from many low growing plants that are grown for their attractive foliage or flowering display.

Many of the plants suitable for this purpose, such as chamomile, pennyroyal and thyme, also have fragrant foliage which is released when the plants are walked upon.

Although grass-free lawns are not as popular as those cultivated from grass, and are not suitable where the lawn needs to be hard wearing such as in children's and pets play area, they are ideal for a small area of a garden to add extra interest all through the year.

Maintenance of a grass-free lawn is usually less than a traditional grass lawn and only needs attention two or three times a year depending on the type of plant used. Many of the plants suitable can be walked on and even mown occasionally to give a level, short sward.

Chamomile *(Chamaemelum nobilis)*

Chamomile has been used in lawns for hundreds of years for its scented foliage. In most cases it is planted on its own to create a chamomile lawn but in other situations it can be mixed with grasses. The latter is ideal where you need the lawn to be more hard-wearing, but still want the fragrance when the lawn is walked on. Chamomile is a perennial plant that is still used as a calming and soothing herb. The type that is used in lawns is a low growing form called 'Treneague' which is a creeping plant with fern-like foliage and does not produce the white daisy-like flowers. Chamomile is tougher than it looks. It is ideal for a small lawn that is used for sitting or sun-bathing on. Mowing and trimming is only needed occasionally.

Thyme *(Thymus serpyllum)*

Thyme is a well known evergreen herb with aromatic foliage that is used for both culinary and medicinal purposes. Many types of thyme are also grown for their attractive pink, mauve or purple flowers that help to attract beneficial insects into the garden. The wild thyme can be grown very easily from seed sown in pots or seed trays and grown on to produce small plants that can be planted out into the prepared area where they will quickly grow to form a dense carpet. Most thyme is naturally spreading in habit and produces small leaves, although a few of the named cultivars have a more upright habit and these are best avoided if you want to keep the thyme lawn as low and compact as possible. There are also many coloured leaved and variegated forms available with different scents and when mixed with green leaved types they create a very colourful and scented lawn.

Thyme can be mown occasionally or trimmed with shears to keep the lawn area in trim. This can be done in early spring just before growth starts and again in mid-summer to trim off the dead flower heads.

Pennyroyal *(Mentha pulegium)*

This is another popular perennial herb that can be used to make a scented lawn. It is a member of the mint family, although it is not used for culinary purposes, unlike other forms of garden mint. Creeping pennyroyal is the variety that is used in lawns, and it has smooth green leaves that give off a strong peppermint scent when bruised. The stems creep along the surface of the ground and root where they touch the soil.

In the past, stems of pennyroyal were used in the house to deter fleas, ants and other insects and it can also be used as a stimulating bath. Very little maintenance is needed to maintain an area of pennyroyal other than an occasional trim.

Clover (*Trifolium repens*)

Clover is usually considered to be a lawn weed but it also makes a very good lawn when planted on its own. It produces attractive leaves with three lobes, remains green all year round due to the fact that it can manufacture its own nitrogen and it also has creamy-white flowers that attract insects and bees.

Another form of clover is 'micro-clover' which is a very low growing and spreading form of white clover that has been developed for use in lawns on its own or mixed with grasses. The even spread of the plant does not create a patchy effect like other clovers and because the leaves are very small they do not dominate the grass species. Trials have shown that lawns that include micro-clover stay greener in dry weather and less nitrogenous fertilizer is needed due to the nitrogen fixing nodules on the roots.

All types of clover are normally sown where they are to grow, either in a new seed bed or over-sown on an existing lawn. Once established they can be mown fairly regularly to keep them short.

Mixed alpines

Alpines are low growing plants that originate from mountainous regions. In a garden they are mainly planted in rock gardens or containers where some are grown for their attractive leaves and others are grown for their flowers. Many types of alpine can be used to create a lawn, such as Sedum, saxifrage, dwarf campanulas, Pratii and Arenaria. These are all naturally low growing spreading plants that will create a carpet of foliage and flowers through the year. Some types can be grown from seed, but the best method of establishing a small alpine lawn is to use pot grown plants. The ground should be prepared as you would for making a lawn and ideally the soil should be free-draining as alpines dislike wet, clay soils. An alpine lawn will need trimming in early autumn to removed dead flowers and should not be walked on too much as some plants have brittle stems and could be damaged. Such a lawn is more decorative than functional.

Heather

Heathers can also be used to make a lawn. There are many different types of heather to choose from, with different flowering seasons and colourful new foliage. Some types need to be grown in acid soils, replicating the conditions found on the heaths and moorlands from which they originate, and others are happy growing in neutral and alkaline soils. Check the pH of your soil before planting.

To keep the plants bushy and compact, they need to be trimmed over just once a year after flowering. A heather lawn is not one that can be walked on a great deal, but it does make a very attractive alternative to a grass lawn.

Bulbs for Naturalizing

Many types of bulbs can be planted in a lawn or a natural area to provide colour and interest. The aim when planting bulbs in a lawn is to try and create a natural effect. For this reason, the bulbs should not be planted in straight rows or blocks. Instead they are normally planted in informal drifts or in groups around the base of trees, where they can be allowed to naturalize and increase in numbers each year.

Spring flowering bulbs are mainly used, although a few autumn flowering types are occasionally planted. In the case of spring bulbs, the grass cannot be cut until around six weeks after flowering or until the foliage of the bulbs has turned yellow and started to die down. This is to allow the bulb time to build up for the following season. With the autumn flowering types, mowing the area where the bulbs are planted should cease in late summer in order to allow the bulbs to grow.

Some types of bulbs naturalize better than others, depending on the location and growing conditions. You also need to think carefully about where you are going to plant. Try to avoid planting in formal, closely mown areas, as after flowering has finished the areas of long grass will spoil the lawn. The best areas to plant in are towards the back of a lawn or where the grass is allowed to grow a little longer, such as a small orchard or a natural, wildflower area. If having areas of longer grass in your lawn is a problem, plant lower growing types of bulbs that flower in later winter or early spring, as by the time the main grass cutting season starts, the leaves of the bulbs will have mostly died down and mowing can continue as normal.

Anemone blanda

This is a lovely low growing, early flowering plant that is ideal for growing around the base of trees and shrubs in a lawn. The daisy-like flowers are produced in late winter and early spring and stand just above the deeply lobed leaves. The overall height of the plant is approximately 15cm (6in) and several named cultivars are available with white, pale blue and violet coloured flowers. The brown knobbly tubers are planted in the autumn and quickly establish to form a large clump.

Colchicum spp. (Autumn crocus)

Autumn crocus is also known as meadow saffron and naked ladies. Although commonly called a crocus, it is not related to the true spring flowering crocus. The corms are planted in early to mid-summer and they produce flowers in early autumn. The goblet-shaped flowers are mainly pink or white and are produced before the leaves, hence 'naked ladies'. After the flowers fade long, broad leaves grow that remain until the following spring.

Crocus spp. (Crocus)

Spring flowering crocuses are very popular in the garden and will grow equally well in a border or in a lawn. Many different colours are available and they can either be grown as a mixture as in single colours. The corms are planted in autumn and the flowers are produced in early to mid-spring. Sizes vary depending on the species being grown but most are between 5–10cm (2–4in). Crocuses naturalize well in a lawn and will after a few years will form dense clumps in spring.

Cyclamen coum

Cyclamen coum is a small hardy plant that flowers from late winter to early spring. The small tubers are planted just below the surface and flowers and leaves are produced at the same time. The small flowers vary from white to shades of pink and the plant grows to approximately 7.5cm (3in) tall. The best situation for this dainty cyclamen is a natural area where the grass is not mown too closely and there is some shade.

Eranthis hyemalis (Winter aconite)

This is another early flowering plant that can be naturalized in lawns. The woody tubers are planted in autumn and in late winter and early spring bright yellow flowers are produced with a collar of green leaves. They grow to approximately 5–7.5cm (2–3in) and are often grown alongside snowdrops. Winter aconites can take a few years to establish, but once they are they will quickly increase to form large areas.

Fritillaria meleagris (Snake's head fritillary)

This bulb is an excellent one to use in a wildflower meadow or easily naturalized in the lawn, especially if the soil is damp. It grows to around 30cm (12in) and throughout the spring produces dainty purple/pink-hanging bell-shaped flowers, and there is also a white form, *Fritillaria meleagris* f. *alba*. Plant the bulbs in situ during the autumn months.

Galanthus nivalis (Snowdrop)

Snowdrops are one of the first bulbs to flower and can often be seen growing through snow in late winter. There are many different types available with single and double flowers and most types will naturalize well in lawns. The bulbs can be planted in autumn but these can be difficult to establish. Alternatively, buy growing plants in spring to establish in the lawn. Their height varies depending on the species or cultivar, but most are between 10–15cm (4–6in) tall.

Hyacinthoides non-scripta (English bluebell)

Bluebells are ideal for naturalizing in wildflower areas or lawns around the bases of trees. They establish very quickly to produce dense clumps. Stalks of scented, bell-shaped, mid-blue flowers are produced in mid- to late spring. In certain soils, bluebells seed very easily and can become a nuisance in borders, so seed heads should be removed to prevent them self-seeding and taking over.

Narcissus (Daffodil)

Daffodils are by far the most popular choice when it comes to planting bulbs in lawns and grass areas. There are many hundreds of different daffodils to choose from and many types can be naturalized in lawns, although it is best to avoid doubles, very dwarf forms and the specialist types. Traditional looking trumpet-shaped flowers look the most natural and many bulb suppliers sell mixtures suitable for naturalizing. The bulbs should be planted in autumn.

Tulipa (Tulipa)

Although not generally planted in lawns, some types of tulip can be used where you want to introduce extra colour in spring. Because tulips are one of the last bulbs to flower in spring, they trend to be planted in natural areas where the grass is allowed to grow longer. Two species that are suitable for naturalizing are *Tulipa sprengeri*, which has orange-red flowers, and the creamy-yellow flowering *Tulipa sylvestris*.

Troubleshooting

The following diagram is designed to help you diagnose conditions suffered by your lawn from the symptoms you can observe. Starting with the part of the lawn that appears to be most affected, by answering successive questions 'yes' [✓] or 'no' [✗] you will quickly arrive at a probable cause. Once you have identified the cause, turn to the relevant entry in the directory of pests and diseases for how to treat the problem.

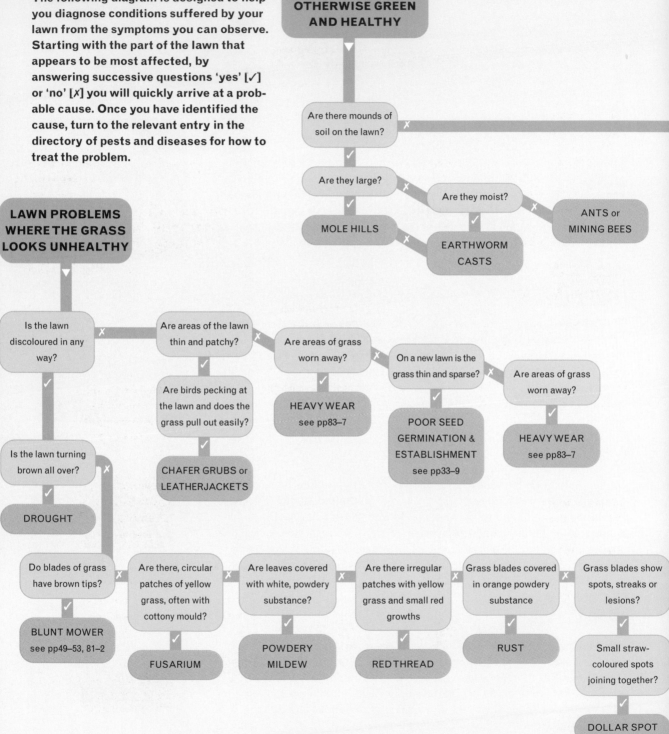

LAWN PROBLEMS WHERE THE GRASS IS OTHERWISE GREEN AND HEALTHY

Are there mounds of soil on the lawn?

Are they large?

MOLE HILLS

Are they moist?

EARTHWORM CASTS

ANTS or MINING BEES

LAWN PROBLEMS WHERE THE GRASS LOOKS UNHEALTHY

Is the lawn discoloured in any way?

Are areas of the lawn thin and patchy?

Are areas of grass worn away?

On a new lawn is the grass thin and sparse?

Are areas of grass worn away?

Are birds pecking at the lawn and does the grass pull out easily?

HEAVY WEAR
see pp83–7

POOR SEED GERMINATION & ESTABLISHMENT
see pp33–9

HEAVY WEAR
see pp83–7

CHAFER GRUBS or LEATHERJACKETS

Is the lawn turning brown all over?

DROUGHT

Do blades of grass have brown tips?

Are there, circular patches of yellow grass, often with cottony mould?

Are leaves covered with white, powdery substance?

Are there irregular patches with yellow grass and small red growths

Grass blades covered in orange powdery substance

Grass blades show spots, streaks or lesions?

BLUNT MOWER
see pp49–53, 81–2

FUSARIUM

POWDERY MILDEW

RED THREAD

RUST

Small straw-coloured spots joining together?

DOLLAR SPOT

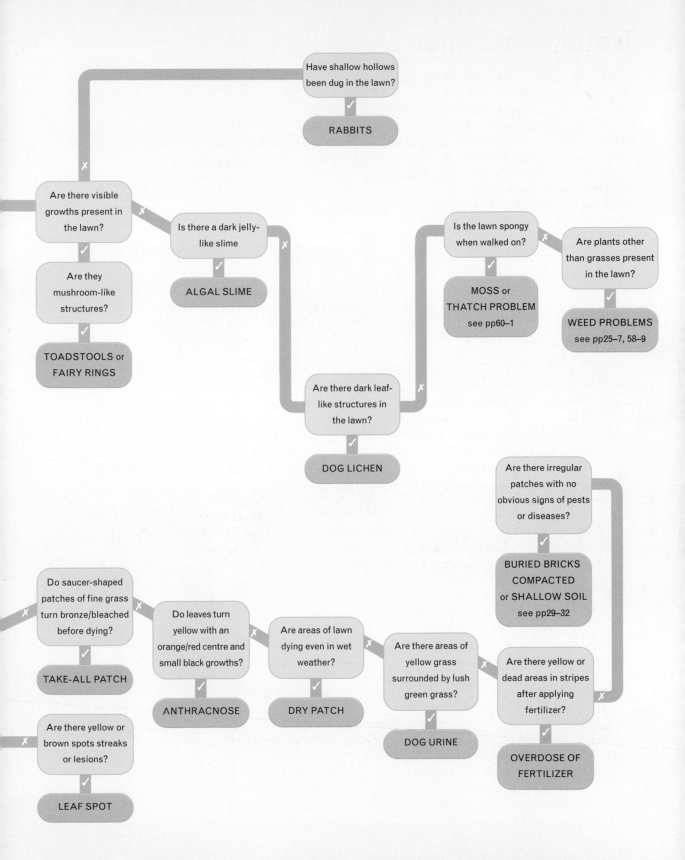

Have shallow hollows been dug in the lawn?

✓ RABBITS

✗ Are there visible growths present in the lawn?

✓ Are they mushroom-like structures?

✓ TOADSTOOLS or FAIRY RINGS

✗ Is there a dark jelly-like slime

✓ ALGAL SLIME

✗ Are there dark leaf-like structures in the lawn?

✓ DOG LICHEN

Is the lawn spongy when walked on?

✓ MOSS or THATCH PROBLEM see pp60–1

✗ Are plants other than grasses present in the lawn?

✓ WEED PROBLEMS see pp25–7, 58–9

Are there irregular patches with no obvious signs of pests or diseases?

✓ BURIED BRICKS COMPACTED or SHALLOW SOIL see pp29–32

Do saucer-shaped patches of fine grass turn bronze/bleached before dying?

✓ TAKE-ALL PATCH

✗ Do leaves turn yellow with an orange/red centre and small black growths?

✓ ANTHRACNOSE

✗ Are areas of lawn dying even in wet weather?

✓ DRY PATCH

✗ Are there areas of yellow grass surrounded by lush green grass?

✓ DOG URINE

✗ Are there yellow or dead areas in stripes after applying fertilizer?

✓ OVERDOSE OF FERTILIZER

✗ Are there yellow or brown spots streaks or lesions?

✓ LEAF SPOT

Pests

Some lawns pests can be serious, whereas others are merely a
nuisance. As there are very few chemical controls available for use
on lawns, cultural and biological controls are the main line of
defence in dealing with the various pests that affect lawns.

Ants

Ants can be a problem in dry summers or in sandy soils but they do very little harm to a lawn.
They do bring soil to the surface, but this is mainly in the summer months and the dry soil can easily
be swept away. Their activities in the soil also means the soil dries out faster and this can lead
to the grass suffering from stress. Many ant killers are available, but to work effectively they
need to be applied to the nest.

Bees

Mining bees can often be found in lawns and they make their nest by digging a small hole down into
the soil where they lay a number of eggs. The first sign that they are in the lawn is usually a small
mound of soil that looks like an ant hill. Mining bees are solitary, very docile and rarely string and
should not be harmed. The damage they do to a lawn is minimal and they are very beneficial
around they garden as pollinators of flowers.

Birds

Birds can often be found pecking and scratching away at the lawn, but they are usually looking for
food in the form of leatherjackets, chafer grubs or ants that are in the lawn. If large amounts of birds
congregate on the lawn, it is usually an indication that there is a pest problem. Occasionally, larger birds
can rip out pieces of grass in search of the grubs, but generally they do little harm and are, in fact,
helping to control the pests.

Chafer grubs

There are several types of chafer grubs and most of them cause
damage on lawns by eating the roots of the grass during the winter
and spring. The 'c' shaped grubs are creamy-white in colour and
approximately 2.5cm (1in) long. They have a dark head and three pairs
of short legs. Chafer grubs tend to be more of a problem in light,
sandy soils and in severe cases they can kill the lawn. Signs that they
are under the lawn is patches of grass dieing and lots of bird visitors
pecking at the lawn. No chemical control is available, but there is a
biological control. This is in the form a nematode that is watered onto
the lawn and is very effective at killing the grubs.

Dogs

Generally, dogs do not cause a great deal of damage unless you have a large energetic dog and
a very small lawn, in which case the grass can be easily ripped up. The urine of bitches, however, does
scorch the grass and leave yellow patches often with green lush grass around them. The yellow
patches are caused by the ammonia in the dog's urine. If at all possible, as soon as you notice the
dog fouling the lawn, dilute the urine with a bucket of water immediately, or train the dog to use
another area of the garden. There are also additives that can be mixed into the dog's food to
reduce this type of scorching of the grass.

Earthworms

There are many types of earthworms but the ones that cause problems on lawns are the ones that produce a cast of soil on the surface. This small mound of soil can make mowing with a cylinder mower difficult and they act as a seed bed for weed seeds. However, the benefits of worms in the soil far outweighs the problems they cause. This is because the deep holes made by worms helps to improve soil drainage, aeration and relieve compaction. The fact that the worms are there is an indication of a good soil. Control is very difficult, as there are no chemical treatments available for soil pests. Worm casts should be brushed off the lawn prior to mowing.

Leatherjackets

Leatherjackets are the larval stage of the crane fly or daddy long-legs. The grey-brown legless grubs are approximately 2.5cm (1in) long and feed on grass roots through the winter and spring before emerging as adults in early autumn. Tell-tale signs are yellow patches or dieing grass and increased bird activity.

Control is by using a nematode that is watered into the lawn in autumn when the eggs have been laid. The nematodes enter the leatherjacket and spread a fungus that stops the grub from eating. Alternatively, the lawn can be soaked with water and covered with black polythene or an old carpet over night. This encourages the leatherjackets to the surface. In the morning when the covering is removed the grubs can be removed by hand.

Moles

Moles can ruin a lawn in a short time by tunnelling just below the surface and by piling up mole hills of soil. In a short time a firm level lawn can be reduces to a bumpy soft lawn. Control is difficult and many of the products that were once available have now been withdrawn. Mole traps set in the runs do work, but they need carefully setting as moles have a very good sense of smell and will easily detect the smell of humans on a trap. Always wear gloves that have been rubbed into the soil first before positioning the trap. Mole deterrents that emit a noise on a regular basis are also available, but their success is varied. Bulbs of a species of allium (onion) planted around the garden are also said to drive away moles from the garden. There are also many other methods that people try such as making vibrations in the soil or placing strong smelling products down the holes, but at the end of the day it is difficult to get rid of them.

Rabbits

The main problem with rabbits is they scratch shallow holes in the lawn to get to the grass roots which they enjoy eating. This is worse in winter when there is little fresh vegetation around. They can also be a problem on newly sown lawns where they will not only scratch holes, but eat the new shoots to ground level. The best method of control is to make the garden rabbit-proof by using wire netting.

Diseases

There are several fungal diseases that attack lawns at various times of the year. Many are encouraged by poor aeration, soil compaction, a build up of thatch and low fertility. In many cases diseases can be prevented or reduced by improving the quality of the lawn by regular maintenance. Unfortunately for the home gardener, chemical control with fungicides is very difficult.

Anthracnose – Collectotrichum graminicola

This disease is mainly associated with annual meadow grass in closely mown lawns, but will also affect rye grass and fescues. It is usually seen from late summer to late winter and appears as yellowing of the leaf which spreads down to the centre of the plant where there may be an orange-red new leaf. Eventually, the base of the plant will develop small, black pin-head structures. This tends to be more of a problem on worn, compacted areas of the lawn, so regular spiking and generally improving the condition of the lawn will help.

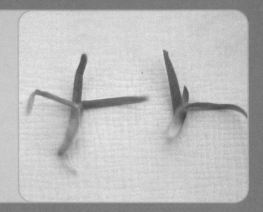

Dollar spot – Sclerotinia homoeocarpa

In recent times, dollar spot seems to be emerging as more of a problem than it used to be. The fungus that causes dollar spot – *Rutstroemia floccosum* (also known as *Sclerotinia homoeocarpa*) – is a fungus that does not produce any spores. This has made identifying this pathogen difficult because most fungi are classified or identified based on the spores they produce. This fungal disease mainly attacks slender creeping red fescue in fine lawns. Small spots approximately 12–25mm (½–1in) across appear and contain bleached or straw-coloured dead grass. The spots can join together to form larger patches. The disease is often associated with warm, humid conditions on lawns that are low in fertility. Good maintenance and regular feeding with improve conditions. Once the disease is present, a systemic fungicide should be used to stop the pathogen that is inside the plant from advancing further.

Dry patch

This is not really a disease as it is not directly caused by a fungal organism. Dry patch causes areas of a lawn to dry out and die, even in wet weather or where the lawn is irrigated. One theory is that fungal mycelium in the soil make the soil water-repellent (hydrophobic) and the grass dies from drought. However, the same mycelium is also found in soils that are not affected. Where areas of dry soil are found in the lawn spiking before irrigating will help the water to soak down to the roots. The addition of a wetting agent or a mild detergent such as washing up liquid added to the water is also beneficial as it helps to reduce the surface tension of the water allowing it to soak in.

Fairy rings – Basidiomycetes

There are three grades of fairy rings, all caused by different types of the fungus *Basidiomycetes*. The worst one kills a circle or arc of grass in the lawn. The second type does not kill the grass but shows up as darker rings of grass, often with toadstools or puffballs growing in it. The third type shows no discolouration to the grass and all that is evident is a ring or part ring of toadstools or puffballs. Control of the first type is very difficult although digging out the affected soil and replacing with new soil does help. The other two types do not kill the grass and feeding with fertilizer or applying sulphate of iron to make the grass darker will help to mask the problem. Any toadstools can be brushed or picked off. There is another type of fairly ring known as a superficial fairy ring. They are caused by various fungi that are present in the thatch layer in for this reason are also called thatch fungi. Areas of grass discolouration may appear mainly during the summer and autumn. Control is the same as other fairly rings.

Fusarium – Microdochium rivale

This is probably the commonest turf disease and tends to attack in spring and autumn. The symptoms are small circular moist patches of yellowing grass and sometimes white or pinkish cottony mould. As the patches increase in size they join to form large areas of dead grass that are slimy to touch. The disease is associated with moist, warm conditions on soft lush grass that may have been given too much nitrogen in early spring or autumn. Bents, fescues and ryegrass are all affected by fusarium. Spiking, scarification to improve air movement around the grass will help, as will the careful use of fertilizer in early spring and autumn.

Leaf spot – Drechslera spp., Bipolaris spp and Curvularia spp

Various fungi can cause leaf spots on grasses and they are very common in warm damp weather. They show as yellow or brown spots, dark streaks or large lesions on the leaves depending on the type of fungi. Most grasses are susceptible to attack but by scarifying, spiking and carrying out general lawn maintenance, leaf spots should not be too much of a problem to control.

Damping-off – Pythium spp., Fusarium spp.

Several different fungi can cause a problem known as damping-off, which is where seedling grasses start to rot off in clumps. The fungi are either soil borne or they can be carried on the seed and they can attack just after germination and while the young grasses are trying to establish. The symptoms occur rapidly and patches of grass will collapse and often turn red, yellow or purple. Both dry and wet soil conditions can favour damping-off as can excessive amounts of fertilizer in the soil. Grass that has been sown too quickly is also likely to be attacked.

To prevent the plants being under stress and vulnerable to attack it is important that good soil preparation is carried out, the seed sowing at the correct density, too much fertilizer is not applied and in dry weather the grass is watered.

Pink Patch – *Limonomyces roseipellis*

This common disease often occurs on its own, but usually it is associated with red thread (see below). The disease looks very similar to red thread, although at closer inspection you will not find the red needles on the blades of grass; instead you might find a white or pink mycelium, cotton-like growth over the leaves, which look white when dry. Pink patch can be found on a wide range of lawn grasses, such as bluegrass, fine fescue, perennial rye grass, and the preventative measures are very similar as with red thread. Fungicide control may help to clear up the disease.

Powdery mildew – *Erysiphe graminis*

This is quite a common lawn disease from late spring until autumn, especially in periods of dry weather. It is very easy to identify as the leaves are covered in a white or grey powdery substance and eventually turn yellow and die. Large infected areas look as if the grass has been dusted with flour or lime. Most grasses can be attacked and the disease tends to be found mainly in lawns where the grass is allowed to grow a little longer or in shade. The powdery mildew fungus grows best in high humidity, low light and cool temperatures. Regular mowing and improving growing conditions will help to reduce the risk of attack.

Red thread – *Laetisaria fuciformis*

Sometime known as corticium, this disease is mainly seen during the summer and autumn months, but it will continue into winter in mild weather. Irregular patches of pale or yellow grass develops and when examined closely you will see small red threads attached to the leaves. Red thread does not kill the grass and is usually found on lawns where fertility is low. Regular feeding will help, although care should be taken not to over-feed, especially in autumn as this may encourage other diseases such as fusarium.

Rust – *Puccinia spp*

Rust diseases are quite specific and will usually only attack one species of grass in a lawn. The first symptoms are yellow spots and flecks on the leaves followed by pustules that release orange spores. Rusts usually occur in warm air temperatures and on plants that are under stress from lack of food or moisture. Regular feeding and general lawn maintenance will greatly reduce outbreaks of the disease.

Take-all patch – *Gaeumannomyces graminis*

This disease is also known as ophiobolus patch and can be serious if you get it in your lawn. It only affects species of agrostis (bent grass) and starts in the summer as small saucer-shaped areas that may be slightly sunken. The grass also takes on a bronzed or bleached colour and eventually the patches can be 30cm (12in) in diameter. As the bent grasses die, other grasses and broad-leaved weeds will colonize the area. The disease is worse on soils with a high pH, where the thatch is thick, fertility is low and drainage is poor. Improving all of these to improve the vigour of the lawn and additional feeding with sulphate of iron to reduce soil pH will help to prevent the disease. Over sowing with red fescue to thicken the sward can also be done as this is not affected by the disease.

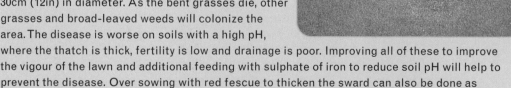

Glossary

Aeration – This is a means of getting air down into the soil to the grass roots or around the base of the grass to promote healthy growth.

Annual – Plants that are annuals grow from seed, flower and produce seed all in one season and then die. They can be grasses and lawn weeds.

Biennial – A biennial takes two seasons to complete its life cycle. The plant develops during the first season and in the second growing season flowers and seed are produced before the plant dies.

Broadcast – A term used to describe a method of sowing seed whereby they are scattered evenly over an area.

Broad-leaved weeds – Weeds growing in lawns other than grasses are classed as broad-leaved.

Bulbils – Small underground organs of several plants such as lesser celandine. These act as food storage during dormant periods and also multiply as a means of increasing the growth of the plant.

Cultivar – A cultivated variety that has been produced by selective plant breeding. In many cases these are improved forms of wild varieties.

Cultivate – When soil is turned over and raked during the preparation of a seed bed.

Cylinder mower – Used to give a close mowing finish. The blades form a cylinder and rotate to cut against a fixed blade in a scissor-like action.

Double digging – Digging is where soil is turned over to the depth of the spade, whereas double digging is where the soil is cultivated to a depth of two spades.

Fertilizer – Substance that can be natural or man-made to supply plants with nutrients needed for growth.

Foliage – Another name for leaves on a plant.

Fruiting bodies – Often found on mosses. These small capsule-like structures contain spores that are released when they are ripe.

Germinate – The point at which a seed starts into growth by producing a tiny root and shoot.

Hoeing – A method of controlling mainly annual weeds by chopping them off at ground level with a flat metal blade on a long handle.

Nutrients – Essential food for plants available in many forms for different parts of the plant.

Pan – A hard layer of soil several inches down that can cause slow drainage or poor root growth.

Perennial – A plant that lives for several years.

Rhizome – An underground spreading root-like stem that produces both roots and shoots.

Rotary mower – A mower with a fast spinning horizontal blade

Rotavator – A machine for turning over soil; sometimes called a mechanical cultivator.

Selective weedkiller – A weedkiller that can determine between grasses and broad-leaved weed in a lawn.

Scarify – To removed plant debris and thatch from the base of a lawn to allow more air to the grass and roots.

Spiking – A method of making holes in a lawn to kelp drainage, relieve soil compaction and to allow air into the soil. Can be done with hollow or solid tines.

Stolons – A horizontal stem that roots at its tip to form a new plant. This new plant in turn produces a stolon and the plant spreads.

Spores – Minute reproductive structures of non-flowering plants such as mosses, ferns and fungi.

Sward – A term used to describe the surface of a lawn.

Swish – A technique used to remove dew from lawns to help prevent damp condition suitable for the growth of fungi and to make mowing easier.

Thatch – A layer of dead plant remains that accumulates on the soil surface to create a spongy layer in the base of a lawn.

Tiller – New shoots produced from close to grown level. Can be encouraged by rolling or mowing.

Tilth – The surface layer of fine, crumby soil created by cultivation.

Turf – A piece of grass that has been grown for transplanting to produce a new lawn. Sometimes called a sod.

Index

Acknowledgements

The author would like to thank Bayer crop science for the use of their images in the Pests & Diseases section. He would also like to thank the following companies that were very helpful in compiling this book:

Q Lawns, Norfolk. Tel. 01842 828266 (www.qlawns.co.uk) for supplying turf and sedum Enviromat.

DLF Trifolium (Johnsons Lawn Seed) Worcestershire. Tel. 01386 793135 (www.dlf.co.uk) for allowing access to photograph their lawn seed trials.

Meadowfield Gardens (www.martinfish.com) for photographic props and assistance with the practical photography.

The publishers would like to thank Coolings Nurseries for their cooperation and assistance with the photography in this book, including the loan of tools and much specialist equipment. Special thanks go to: Sandra Gratwick. Coolings Nurseries Ltd, Rushmore Hill, Knockholt, Kent, TN14 7NN. Tel: 00 44 1959 532269; Email: coolings@coolings.co.uk; Website: www.coolings.co.uk.